The Winds of Change

A Guided Journey with Healing Music through Grief, Loss & Transformation

by

MARCIA BREITENBACH

Design and layout by Richard Diffenderfer

Printed by Vaughan Printing, Nashville, TN

ISBN 0-9670507-4-X

First Printing, August 2002

Printed in the United States

About the Cover

THE TITLE OF THIS AMAZING, HEALING PAINTING by Michael Ives is "My Angels." When we are visited by the winds of change, we can be sure that our angels are right there, hovering outside our door and our heart, waiting to assist us in our transformation. I believe that all we need to do is to invite them in and ask for their help.

Here is the magical story of "My Angels." I met a woman at the Johrei Center wearing a periwinkle t-shirt with a picture of three angels hovering outside a barrio door, done in bright, southwestern colors. I told her how beautiful and healing the image was and asked her where I could get the shirt for myself and my clients.

Her name was Sara and she related the wondrous way the angels brought this shirt to her. Five years ago, Sara found out she had breast cancer. Her friend saw the shirt on a stranger and asked where the woman had gotten the shirt so that she could get one for her friend Sara. The woman, Amber, took the shirt off her back and gave it to her to give to Sara.

It helped Sara through difficult times. Sometime later, she gave it to her friend, Maureen, who had just been diagnosed with stage 3 breast cancer. Maureen is now fine, but last year, Sara had a recurrence. She e-mailed Maureen in Guam and asked her to mail the shirt back. It has now seen Sara through almost nine months of chemo and she is in remission.

I told Sara that I would try to locate the artist so we could get more shirts. Little did I know that he is a celebrated artist in Tucson, and that his studio is within a few minutes drive from my house! My family and I went to see him the next day. We loved his work and commissioned a painting for our home, based on the original design of "Angels at My Door," the picture on the shirt.

The cover of this book is the result of this. This image is so appropriate for anyone undergoing a major change: it is a powerful symbol to remind us of the unseen helpers we all have, but sometimes forget about.

Acknowledgments

I would like to express my deep appreciation and gratitude to:

God, for the lessons you give to me, your guidance, and for the opening of my heart;

My angels and guides for their love, and for bringing this music through me;

Myself, for being willing to *listen* for guidance and for making the commitment to becoming fully alive and an instrument for peace;

My sweet family, Howie, Alice, Pepper, Betsy and Sky, who love and encourage me, and are gentle witnesses to the everyday challenges of becoming *myself*;

My ancestors and my wonderful parents who gave me life and opportunities to learn and to grow; my sister in the spirit world and my sister on this earthly plane for their loving support of their "eccentric little sister;"

My friends who support my transformation on all levels, who gently nudge me to take action when I become stuck, and who are beautiful, incredible mirrors of my growth;

Richard Diffenderfer for his artful formatting and design for this book and Chris Howell for her editing skills;

Gillian DeLear for her superb ear and patience with my learning curve in the recording studio;

The musicians who brought their talents and spirit to this music; the children who sang about rainbows and bridges, bringing their sweetness and playfulness to this project;

Michael Ives, visionary and artist, for his transformative and healing artwork for the cover of this book;

All the clients, friends and family members over the years who have weathered the winds of change and shared their challenges and triumphs with me;

And to you, the reader and listener, for your courage to walk a healing path through your life storms, being ever so compassionate and gentle with your soul's progress. —*MB*

The Winds of Change

A Guided Journey with Healing Music
through Grief, Loss & Transformation

Contents

Introduction 1

    Grief is Energy 5

Step One

Begin from a Place of Power: I am on a Journey
of Re-Creation and Transformation 7

    Lisa and Sarah 11

    My Brain is a Powerful Tool for Healing 12

    I Use Intention, Music and Affirmations for Healing 14

    AFFIRMATION 1 16

    SONG: *"The Winds of Change"* .17

Step Two

Be a Bridge for Healing: I Connect Daily with
My Inner and Outer Resources 16

    I Build Bridges of Support for This Re-Birth 16

    SONG: *"We Are All Rainbows"* .20

AFFIRMATION 2 21

I Build a Bridge to My Spiritual Self & Spiritual Helpers 21

SONG: *"The Voice of the Twilight"* .26

I Park Myself on My Porch 27

AFFIRMATION 3 28

I Build a Bridge to My Human Helpers 28

Pets are Powerful Resources and Healers 30

Nature is the #1 Healer 30

SONG: *"Nature's Gifts"* 33

AFFIRMATION 4 34

A Visual Tool: I Make a Resource Mandala 34

Step Three

I Surrender to, Trust and am Grateful for this Journey 36

I Relax Into This Journey 36

Fear No Longer Rules Me 39

I Let Go of Old Baggage 39

SONG: *"What's Stopping You?"* .40

SONG: *"I Surrender"* 43

I Live My Life's Purpose 45

AFFIRMATION 5 47

I Can Have Gratitude for My Misfortunes 47

I Create a Better Balance of Positive and Negative Self-Talk . . .50

AFFIRMATION 6 52

Step Four
I Learn to Accept and Love All Parts of Myself 54

SONG: *"Learning to Love Myself"* .55

SONG: *"To Be Gentle With Myself"* 56

My Shadow or Dark Side Isn't So Dark After All 56

AFFIRMATION 7 58

Step Five
I Make Life-Affirming Choices Daily Which Create
More Balance 58

I Reduce Guilt in My Life 58

SONG: *"Should'ng on Myself"* .60

I Choose Love More Than Fear 61

AFFIRMATION 8 65

I Support the Lightness in my Being 65

SONG: *"Light in My Soul"* 66

AFFIRMATION 9 67

I Can be Kind or Mean 67

SONG: *"Sticks and Stones"* 69

AFFIRMATION 10 70

I Can Expand or Contract 70

I Choose Color as a Healing Tool .72

I Use Music, TV, Sound, Breath and Movement Consciously
for my Healing Journey 73

AFFIRMATION 11 77

I Contemplate the Mysteries of Life 77

SONG: *"The Mystery of Life"* 79

AFFIRMATION 12 81

Step Six
I Tend My Soul's Garden Daily 81

SONG: *"Beautiful"* 82

I Listen for Inner Guidance 83

I Mend My Fences 83

I Make Choices for Growth 84

I Cultivate Compassion and Patience for My Growth 84

AFFIRMATION 13 87

A Review 87

I Become an Angel on Earth 88

CD Credits 92

Introduction

I KNOW A LOT ABOUT WIND because I grew up in Wyoming. For all of you who have either lived in Wyoming or stayed there long enough to take a good look, you know what I'm talking about. In Casper, my hometown, it's windy nearly every day. I was talking to someone a few years ago about Wyoming and she asked, "Did you ever notice that the people who live there don't have any lips?" I laughed and said that no, I really hadn't, and asked to what she attributed that little-known fact. She replied, "The wind, of course." I went home and peered at my lips in the mirror, deciding, "Hmmm, a little thin, perhaps, but I *do* have lips, thank God." I began to think about all the other people I knew growing up whose lips where whittled away by the merciless daily winds.

Wind not only wears things down, but it moves things around. It doesn't bypass anything or anyone. If it's a big wind, it can rip a sign off its post and send it sailing, knock things over that break into little pieces, and send human beings running for cover. On the other hand, little winds can feel like gentle feathers brushing your skin, or short unexpected gusts that rustle your hair and leave you feeling slightly confused.

Change and wind have a lot in common. Some of the gentle breezes of change that come into our lives, such as the arrival of a dear old friend for a visit, are welcome and bring joy and delight. Others are like the proverbial hurricane and leave us frightened and faced with chaos and a lot of rebuilding. This book is about the gales and turbulence that come with big change.

The day of major change looks like any other day. You wake up and look outside and see nothing that even hints at the intensity and inevitability of what is to follow. This is a day that will alter who you are forever, and yet there is no banner across the sky that proclaims this *rite of passage.*

For that is indeed what major change is in your life. *It is a rite of passage, a time when you are leaving behind what is familiar and comfortable, and entering a place that may contain dark and unfamiliar corners. It is a moving toward the unknown and becoming someone different than you were before the winds of change arrived.* Perhaps this is the day that a loved one dies, or you receive a diagnosis of a serious life-threatening illness. You may be involved in a life-or-death accident or assault, or you are presented with divorce papers. This could be the day you lose your job or financial support. Perhaps the change you are dealing with did not arrive on one certain day. It may have been a gradual process, such as aging, a debilitating illness, or menopause.

Whatever the agent of change is, you have been handed a ticket to *transformation.* This may not be a ticket that you purchased willingly, yet it is a journey that is now yours. You have the possibility of walking and guiding your healing journey with powerful tools and intention. This book is about giving you healing guidelines to not only manage the major changes and losses that you are facing now or will face in the future, but also to move forward into your new self and life. *All major change provides a wake-up call to evaluate our lives and priorities. It is a time of inner awakening. You are given steps here to assist this awakening. You can become more comfortable with change, have less fear about the inevitable metamorphoses that occur, and feel empowered to make daily choices that will lead you to healing and wholeness.*

If you're like me, when something like this happens, you just want to "wake up from this nightmare" so that "everything can be the same as it was." We humans do not like change! It doesn't matter how well we understand intellectually that change is inevitable. When it happens, we are unprepared and we may flounder for quite some time before we "find our feet" again. From my years of personal as well as professional work with grief and loss, I have selected the attitudes and avenues that seem to help those who have been most resilient when facing major change. I include parts of their stories to illustrate the steps for change and transformation outlined in this book. The songs I have written bring these tools and frames of reference to a deeper level—consciously as well as subconsciously.

Reflection

Major change is a rite of passage, a time when you are leaving behind what is familiar and comfortable, and entering a place that may contain dark and unfamiliar corners. It is a moving toward the unknown and becoming someone different than you were before the winds of change arrived.

Using the principles in this book pro-actively, along with the supporting songs, can allow you to *confidently move with change*, rather than become overly stressed, feel controlled by forces outside of yourself and a victim of your circumstances.

Each one of us can travel the road of transformation with awareness and choice. So many of us make an unconscious choice to be a victim to its ups and downs. When the wind of change comes at us, we use our energy to brace against it, hoping it will pass quickly. We allow ourselves to be blown back and forth, up and down by the tempest of the experience and our emotions. We lack a safe and structured container as well as resources and meaning for our voyage of healing. It is my intention to show you a way to respond *empowered* to all your life's challenges. It is a path of awareness, of conscious choice, and of using the *energy* of this event, no matter how tragic, to put the pieces of yourself and your life back together in a new way. This perspective can allow you to bend rather than break from the strain and stress of resisting the change. And, this path can bring you closer to being who you were meant to be, becoming your true *self*.

Join me on this journey. Give yourself time to ponder the steps I suggest in this book and the music I have written which supports each step on your way to self-healing. The songs come from my personal healing journey, as well as from my professional work. The music and affirmations, numbered and in bold type, are intended to be used as aids to help you form stronger pathways to healing and more integrated and life-affirming connections in your brain through repetition. They will assist you in forming a strong, safe and nurturing container for your time of healing. Take the music with you in your car and play it as you might a self-help tape. Some of the songs will touch you more than others, depending on what your personal issues are. Those who have used my music on their healing journeys have reported that when they play repeatedly the songs with which they resonate the most, they notice greater peace, and trust of the process. In addition, if you can begin to sing along, their ability to help you heal will increase because you bring them into yourself and generate the tones and words, rather than just being in a receptive mode. **Never underestimate the power of a song, *sung with your own voice*, to initiate inner change.**

Whether you are in the midst of a life crisis or change, or are enjoying a period of stability and have only the minor challenges of daily living to contend with, you can take time to try on this perspective and to see what parts of it fit you. I believe we don't need life crises to initiate healing, because, in truth, every moment of each day is an opportunity to move towards wholeness. It's all in how we look at each moment and in the choices we make. As with everything you read, you bring your life experiences, your particular style of discernment and critical attitude to the thoughts and words I have written. Take what speaks to your spirit, mind, body and heart, and put it into action.

Grief is Energy

Every change in life, from the minor to more catastrophic ones, brings losses. *It is how we look at these losses and changes that can make the difference between becoming a victim of change and grief energy, or learning how to channel this energy to higher purposes.*

We are often taught, by example, to fear change and loss. It is the "big, bad wolf at the door," ready to turn our lives inside out. Sometimes we just want to run and hide under the covers until the wolf goes away. Or we can run out the back door and change addresses. Somehow that wolf is always smarter than me and seems to find me at my new location. Over time, I've changed my perspective rather than my "address."

My view of grief is this: Grief is neither bad nor good. It is simply a response to change and loss, and it is *energy*. It is *how we receive and process this energy that makes all the difference in the world.* Instead of bracing against and fearing grief energy, you can look at your healing process differently, trust it, and use your intention to transform the experience and your life in positive ways.

Some of my clients are overwhelmed by their pain and feel hopeless that their feelings and circumstances will ever change. They are paralyzed at times with the intensity of their loss and their brain is stuck on a circuit that contains some of the following messages: They are incompetent with their grief... They are alone with their grief... They will either go crazy, die or fall apart if they allow themselves to fully feel their feelings... They are guilty of somehow causing this loss... And, because they are in such a "bad place," they contaminate or cause harm to their relationships. In short, they feel "less than" at the same time that they have all the horrible feelings that

Reflection

Grief is neither bad nor good. It is simply a response to change and loss, and it is energy. It is how we receive and process this energy that makes all the difference in the world. We can brace against the wind, or we can dance with it.

come with loss.

Feelings of inadequacy, of being "less than" or "not good enough," are a core issue that human beings carry. I believe it is at the root of most of the conflict between people and countries. When we go through major challenges and losses, this core issue is activated. View it as an incredible opportunity to tackle the issue head on and use it in your self-transformation! "Oh right," said one client, "you expect me to dive into this self-love/hate thing while I'm in the midst of my life falling apart? I already feel bad enough!" "Precisely," I replied, "how much worse can it get? Look at this as God's gift of a makeover. Kind of like they do on Oprah." (My humor is lost on some of my clients.)

Put on a different pair of glasses to look at another way to move through grief. Think of this approach as a grief makeover where you are *rebuilding yourself from the inside out*. I will outline 6 steps to meet change with confidence and a structure to assist you in having a more balanced and purposeful transforming experience. Thus, when you have a date with the big C, and I'm not necessarily referring to cancer, but rather to *Change*, you will be able to bend like the willow. You will not be broken by the winds of change. First, walk with me upon part of my journey.

Step One

Begin from a Place of Power —
I am on a Journey of Re-Creation and Transformation

One of my days of *Change* began on a beautiful cloudless summer morning in Colorado. I was going to take some time to hike and have a picnic lunch before my shift at work later that afternoon. I wanted to be in nature, a place where I felt whole, happy, and at peace. However, on this day I was stalked by a stranger whose actions would change the course of my life.

I had followed a trail for a short ways and then took off cross-country. Normally I am a model hiker and don't veer off the trails so as not to harm the plants beneath my feet. Yet, on this day, I wanted to get to an obscure place in as short a time as possible. I wanted a quiet place off the beaten track where I would be alone and undisturbed by other hikers. I crossed a fence line and found a secluded spot on a hillside that had sun and shade, a place to sit that was fairly comfortable, and all the quiet a soul could ask for. I sat there for a good half-hour, reading my book, eating my lunch, and letting go of the stresses of my daily life. I heard a twanging sound and thought it must be the wind on the barbed-wire fence below. A few moments later, however, I heard footsteps coming towards me. As I looked up from my book, I saw a large man approaching.

The minutes that followed seemed endless yet at the same time happened very quickly. Before I could even get up, he was upon me and cut off my screams with his hand. The terror of such an event is unbelievable. I was sure I was going to die. During the agonizing minutes that followed, I found that my physical strength and my classes in self-defense did not assist me to disengage my attacker. I could not believe this was happening. At some point I was able to shove him off balance and to free myself enough to run screaming down the hillside. I had the presence of mind to yell as if I were calling to a friend who was nearby, which scared him off in the other direction. And yet, my ordeal was not over. I was running naked and barefoot over desert-like country, in the hot sun, with the possibility of being assaulted again by someone else. I stopped and felt fairly certain I was not being followed. I attempted to re-trace my steps back to the hillside where my clothing and belongings were but could not find them. I began my trek back to civilization and safety over rough terrain and hot rocks. I was terrified of being seen, and yet I needed to be seen to get help. After about two hours, I made it to the main road into the hiking area. I hid behind a big rock and prayed for God to send me a woman. Moments later a woman jogger came right by my rock and I called out to her. She was the first angel in my healing.

I felt shattered by my experience, as if I had been blown to bits that were scattered everywhere. I didn't know who I was anymore, other than a mass of raw and powerful feelings. One reason we become overwhelmed by grief at these times is because we are dealing with multiple losses. In my case, there was the initial loss of innocence, of feeling that I was safe in my place of solace, nature. Other losses that I susequently had to face were the loss of trust, confidence, self-worth and faith. I couldn't imagine that I would ever feel whole again and not in pain. Herein lies the first part of step one.

Even as you are grappling with feelings of shock and disbelief, or a multitude of strong emotions, it is important to **acknowledge** to yourself that the winds of change are blowing through your life and that you have been placed upon a path of transformation. Of course, when you are in the initial stages of loss as a result of change, you are not usually looking for hidden gifts and possibilities. You are looking for a way out of the pain. But that is the old way of dealing with loss. I am asking you to don that different pair of glasses for a bit and see that major changes, such as the assault I personally endured, allow for the possibility of self re-creation. Why not? What is the most you can lose by doing so? And, more importantly, what might you gain?

This step is crucial because such events bring strong emotions with them. *If we react only by becoming identified with these feelings and being at their mercy, we send a distinct message to ourselves that we can't handle what has happened, that we are the victim of our change and loss, and that we don't expect much from this other than heartbreak and misery.*

I am not suggesting that you suppress your feelings of grief. In fact, it is by allowing an expression and acknowledgment of *all* your feelings that true healing can happen. What I *am* suggesting is that you can be feeling all the tumultuous emotions that you have in each moment, and *at the same time,* you can be giving yourself messages of empowerment about the transformation process that accompanies change. "I feel like I am having a nightmare that I can't wake up from. I can't imagine ever feeling normal or good again. *And, at the same time, I am willing to acknowledge that this crisis has brought the possibility of re-defining myself and re-shaping my life out of this place of being broken.*"

Of course, the makeover I refer to is an internal one that necessitates letting go of some aspects of the self and rearranging others. Although you may find yourself in pieces after your loss, and are in fact going through a death of your old "self," you have the opportunity to put yourself back together in any way that suits you. Unlike Humpty Dumpty who was unable to pick up his pieces, you have the ability to not only rebuild yourself, but *to do so with the intention of creating someone better than you were.* It is possible. But if you want to become the magnificent being you were meant to be, it is important to undertake this process with great care. Also know that how you speak about your life and losses will define how the journey manifests.

Reflection

The healing journey is about balance. Feel all the tumultuous emotions that you have in each moment, and at the same time, give yourself messages of empowerment about the transformation process that accompanies change.

Lisa and Sarah

While a hospice bereavement counselor I worked with a family whose matriarch had died. This mother's two adult daughters had very different grieving experiences. Both daughters were hit hard by their mother's illness and death. Lisa, the younger daughter, acknowledged early on that she knew she was going to be changed by the loss. "I feel like I have been blown to bits and pieces by Mom's death. I don't know who I am anymore. I'm no longer in that role of caregiving. Am I still a daughter? My routine is gone. I feel adrift on the ocean. I also sense that I am going to be a different Lisa down the road. I want to grow and learn from this death and my grief." Sarah, the eldest, spoke of her mother's death: "I can't deal with this. This is too much. I just want my life back the way it was." Sarah refused support from myself and her family and did her best to return her life to what she had before her mother died. She would not talk about her mother, her feelings or other's grief. Seven months after the death, Sarah's marriage and family life fell apart. She was not successful in restoring herself and life to the "way it was."

You will never be the exact person you were before the day of change. You need time to grieve the things you have lost. At the same time, recognize that there may be benefits to being changed, although they *may not be apparent until you are much further along your healing path.*

So often before we are visited by these life-changing losses, we move through each day with habitual routines, placing priority on the physical and material aspects of our existence. Then, our private earthquake hits us, and we are shattered. It seems to take major change for us humans to "shake out" beliefs and activities that no longer serve us and begin to redefine who we are and what is truly important. Who we *really* are is not the part of us that is self-defined as a mother, brother, sister, a grocery clerk or a minister; it's not the part of us that is shy or extroverted, our age or physical condition; who we really are cannot be defined in those terms. Since each of us will go through this shattering process at least one time in our lives, why not make the choice to build someone more loving, more aware, more involved with life, or whatever you desire for yourself?

The first step of the process is to acknowledge you are on a path of transformation and to state your intention to use the energy of change to re-create yourself in positive ways. By doing so, you begin your journey of healing from a position of power. Whatever the change is, it is accompanied by various losses. This could be the loss of health, a loved one, or a way of life. Grief is our response to loss and includes a multitude of feelings. Everyone knows what grief feels like, although not each person responds to grief energy in the same way. You will still have your individual responses, *but by declaring that you will not be a victim to this force and that you recognize it as energy which can be productive and positive, you create a shift in how your entire being processes it.* You can have a different experience if you so choose.

I Use My Brain as a Powerful Tool for Healing

How you talk to yourself about your experience defines what kind of journey you will have. Remember how the two sisters spoke of their loss? Lisa's language reflected a feeling of empowerment: "I want to grow and learn." Sarah's voice came from feeling overwhelmed: "I can't deal with this." Ultimately in the "bigger picture," I think both women were on the journey each was meant to be on. Yet, given the choice, I would choose the path that offers less fear, resistance and more mastery and redemption for my suffering. I want the path that leads to feeling more whole in my spirit, mind, body and heart. Your soul's desire is to be whole and healed. In order to survive and thrive from your life challenges, you must use the incredible power of your brain! This is a big stretch for me, as I feel my brain is shrinking as I get older. Just keeping track of day-to-day details is becoming a challenge! (This is a good example of how *not* to talk to yourself...If I continue to tell myself that I'm barely competent at handling everyday life, I increase the chance of these challenges occurring). It is your thoughts about the changes in your life, what you say to yourself about your ability to handle them, and what you say out loud to others that inform the healing process. Your brain transmits these messages inwardly and outwardly. It can be a mighty ally in your journey. Use it! *Consciously decide* that you will take the time to "program" your journey toward positive transformation. Once you have made this decision, you will find that you can re-frame your experiences toward a path of purpose and meaning rather than one that feels hopeless, out-of-control and void of meaning.

Reflection

It is your thoughts about the changes in your life, what you say to yourself about your ability to handle them, and what you say out loud to others that inform the healing process.

A wonderful way to reinforce your choice to use intention for healing is to add "conscious questioning" to each step. This is simply a question directed at the self that gets to the heart of the matter. For example, with *Step One*, you might ask yourself, "What messages am I giving myself today about my situation?" "Is this the message I want to be living?" Awareness of our thoughts assists us in making our choices for healing. By confronting ourselves, these questions present the opportunity to be honest, rather than accept the status quo that may have become comfortable. They provide a form of self-permission for reaching for that which may be better for us.

I Use Intention, Music and Affirmations for Healing

This conscious use of *intention* is the beginning of an integrated system of healing and transformation. You will be presented with six steps to an empowered and balanced journey. Each step requires you to take a powerful stance and to look at your process with a different set of glasses. What I mean by "taking a stance" is that you are stating from a position of power that you will live your journey with *intention* and *purpose*. Each step, on its own, may not appear "new" to you. You will find that as you use your intention more consciously—through the affirmations and your response to the music—you will engage a part of your brain that will allow you to transform your grief energy into life energy. Allow the music and your "Words of Power," the affirmations, to bring you to a place of strength, of feeling more like you are responding rather than reacting to your life challenges.

Intention is a concept that may require some definition. Intention is " a determination to act in a certain way; a purpose, aim, end," or so states my Merriam-Webster dictionary. Many people have discovered over the years that if they keep a clear intention, then what they hope to accomplish happens with less resistance and more ease. By using these steps, you will discover that you feel more energized, that your purpose and meaning in your life increase, and you can experience a profound sense of gratitude for each day.

It can be helpful to state your intention in writing and then to say it to yourself daily. Speaking the words out loud is even better than just saying them to yourself, because you are engaging another sense—your ears—and you are also putting it out into the Universe in a more definitive way. Sharing your intentions with a loved one takes this process even further. You will feel more commitment to your goal if you tell another person what it is.

If you want to get the most from this functional tool, use your full body to support your intention. Stand on both feet, preferably barefooted so that your feet can have a better connection with the floor. Allow your knees to remain soft and breathe from your belly. Voice your statements of power with a soft focus, but with a strong voice. Take a deep breath after each affirmation and allow it to settle into your being. You may also choose to move with your affirmations or to dance them. Play and experiment, for by doing so, you create more choices for yourself.

Although I am giving you various affirmations throughout this book that can be used to express your intentions, they are a springboard from which to create your own. These statements are very potent and if they are said in your own way, they will carry more of your self to God and your other resources. Make sure they fit you. Feel free to use one temporarily until you find one that suits you better. They are merely a way to connect you to the power source available to you at all times.

Some people hesitate to use affirmations because they don't fully believe them. Don't worry, some part of you does, and it will use the statement to create a more powerful and positive belief system that will serve you better. It is important to use them daily, or as close to daily as you can manage. You can copy them on 3x5 cards and tape them to the mirror in your bathroom. If possible, draw an image that goes along with the words you have chosen. The power of a symbol combined with words will stimulate more than one area of the brain and increase the statement's ability to effect change from within. Put the affirmations where you will see them and can then repeat them to yourself at least twice a day. Some people put them on the refrigerator, which is OK if you don't have much else on it. But if there are other things posted there, you are less likely to see it. Also, if your mind is on that last piece of chocolate cake inside, guess which thought will carry the most weight! Wherever you place it, take the time to read it, or it will not serve its powerful purpose. Through repetition, you are creating new pathways in your brain and the healing beliefs that can replace or at least offset some of the limiting and negative beliefs you may be harboring.

AFFIRMATION 1: **I am not a victim to the energies of change and my grief. I will use this transformational energy to heal and to re-create and re-build myself to be the person I was meant to be, to become the best me possible!**

The song, *"Winds of Change,"* is about transformation through difficult loss, and the hope of not only surviving the grief process, but of emerging more whole and more fully who one is meant to be. Breathe deeply as you listen to it.

I have found that the process of *"re-membering"* oneself, or putting back together the pieces which were *"dis-membered"* by the life challenge, to be a life-long path. It is one that brings great satisfaction at each juncture in the road when I make choices that connect me more deeply with my soul and the divine spark within.

Step Two

Be a Bridge for Healing: I Connect Daily with My Resources

The previous song about change contains the promise of survival, partially as the result of "not being alone" with the challenge or loss.

Are there times when you feel all alone and that nobody could possibly understand what you are going through? This is the way most people feel at some point during their grief process. On one level, it is true. No other human being can get through your pain for you and no one can truly understand what you are going through because they are not fully in your particular circumstances and life experience.

However: *You are not alone in your grief. You have comfort and resources every step along the way.* And this is an important stand for you to take in order to go through your grief in a more conscious and productive way. We often don't remember this truth, yet it is crucial.

The second step in the process is to acknowledge that you are not alone and to ask for help. You must strengthen your bridges or connections to your inner and outer resources.

I Build Bridges of Support for this Re-Birth

You are going through a *life transformation* process when you grieve. It is not unlike the birthing process. You are "birthing" a new

The Winds of Change

The winds of change blow through
    my life,
What I had has been taken away.
Will I ever feel like I'm whole again,
I can only live day by day.

CHORUS:

And I will get through this time,
    for I'm not alone,
On days when I'm feeling low,
    these words bring me home,
Within every challenge I face,
There's a purpose that's part of
    a bigger plan,
And I am transformed by your grace,
I'm more fully who I AM.

This journey is hard and it tests my faith,
Parts of me feel so broken and gone,
I'm picking up the pieces now,
And I'm choosing to heal and go on.

I take the time to rebuild myself,
And to see who I'm meant to BE,
With Grace and Love,
I am coming home,
I am grateful for re-membering me.

The winds of change blow through
    my life,
Who I am's still a mystery to me,
I'm on a path to heal myself,
To find wholeness that sets me free.

Reflection

You are going through a life transformation *process when you grieve. It is not unlike the birthing process. You are "birthing" a new you and it is a challenging time.*

Reflection

We are each a bridge, just like a rainbow is a bridge that brings together the sky and the earth. You can build bridges to your resources— to God and nature and to other helpers in "spirit form," to your inner self and to other humans. As you make the effort to do this daily, you will then witness an abundance of love and miracles in your life.

you and it is a challenging time. We don't expect a mother to go through this process alone. I am so grateful for the many resources I had during the pregnancy and birth of my daughter such as midwives, family and friends, physicians and others who helped to support me. They assisted in the bridging of my inner resources for the journey through encouragement and sharing their skills and their experience.

What resources am I referring to for your re-birthing experience? They are God, spiritual helpers like angels and guides, your inner Higher Self, other human beings, the natural world, and the things and activities which support and nourish you. That's a lot of help! Sadly, while we are in the midst of crisis and change, many of us cut ourselves off from a fair amount of this support. And yet, it is available to us at all times, no matter how deeply we are grieving.

Harriet's husband died from cancer after a prolonged illness. Harriet had lived through life-threatening experiences as a youngster and knew that when "the going gets tough, you reach out for some help." She reached deep inside and began to take time every day to pray and meditate. She called her friends and family who were supportive and asked each one of them to assist her in specific ways. "Now, Sue's my walking friend. We take a walk in the desert every week together. Bonnie is my sewing friend. She comes over here on Tuesdays." She joined a grief support group for a period of time. She began to journal her feelings as they did in the support group. "I feel like I'm taking my healing into my own hands, and it makes me feel stronger," she said. "I know that if I don't make a concerted effort to stay connected, I will land in a big black hole."

After the death of my mother and the assault, I think I chose the big black hole. But by default, mind you, as I didn't know there was another way. To my credit, I made conscious efforts to connect with friends and therapy. Music began to pour into me and assisted me in making a stronger connection to my spirit. The song that follows speaks to the importance of making inner and outer connections.

One day I was missing a loved one who had died and gone to "The Other Side." I stood on my porch after a heavy monsoon, facing the Catalina Mountains, when my gaze shifted to the right. I beheld a fantastic rainbow, which seemed to reach out to me with its shimmering colors. As I gazed at its beauty, I heard the words, "You can be a bridge too," in my head. And, the words to this wonderful

We are all Rainbows

Connected to our inner Light,
Love dwells within,
Connected to our inner Voice,
Healing begins.

We are all Rainbows, Bridges of Love,
Made of all colors,
And lit from Above.
We are all Rainbows, spanning
*   the skies,*
Reaching towards Heaven,
Radiant as Sunrise.

Rainbows are bridges, that connect
*   Earth to Sky,*
They can teach us to make, that
*   Connection inside.*
We each have the power, to build
*   bridges for healing,*
Making Heaven on Earth, in our
*   hearts and our lives.*

song were born.

We are each a bridge, just like a rainbow is a bridge that brings together the sky and the earth. You can build bridges to your resources—to God and nature and to other helpers in "spirit form," to your inner self and to other humans. As you make the effort to do this daily, you will then witness an abundance of love and miracles in your life.

Let me reaffirm the importance of using intention to assist in the building of your bridges. By stating your intentions, you are acknowledging your situation and are putting yourself in a position to *walk* your healing journey, rather than be dragged down the path kicking and screaming. You announce that you are willing to send forth your energy to connect with that which will assist your healing process. You are *not* choosing a victim position.

> AFFIRMATION 2: **I am not alone. I build bridges to the resources available to me that assist me in navigating my journey with grace, meaning, more joy and purpose.**

At those times during your day when you feel alone and over-whelmed, take a breath and tell yourself, "Oh yes, although I am *feeling* alone and very sad at this moment, I have help and love available to me right now. I can call on this help whenever I want. I can build a bridge to assist me in healing myself."

Part of the power you bring to your journey is an ability to shift your perspective slightly, as if you were looking at a landscape in a picture frame. Imagine taking just the frame and looking through it at the landscape to your right. That is what you can do with your words and intentions when faced with difficult times. You are re-framing the picture you see. Let's return to building bridges to your resources.

I Build a Bridge to My Spiritual Self & Spiritual Helpers

Your most important bridge is to your spiritual self. Without a conscious connection to God, you will be more likely to become a victim to your grief.

Let's talk about God for a moment. I grew up believing that if you want to get along with people you don't discuss two things: God and politics. I can certainly leave politics out of this book, but not God.

Grief is always a spiritual experience in some way. How does this apply if you don't believe in God? If you feel you have no connection to God, let me ask you to consider the following: Do you love going to natural places like the mountains or the ocean? Do these places give you a feeling of peace, awe or reverence? Do you feel renewed by being there? Or, how about the feeling you get when you hold a baby or your pet and gaze into their adoring eyes? Do you feel connected to something bigger than you? Does the beauty of a flower arrangement take away your breath and make you feel better inside? These are all expressions of God or Spirit. God is about feeling connected to something outside yourself or having feelings of peace and renewal, among other things. So, although you may label these experiences differently, we all share them. What name you call God is not important. Use your intention to connect with this resource each day and you are well on your way to feeling more whole and at peace with your situation. *Even people who feel they are already deeply religious or spiritual need to consciously make this intention daily, since old patterns of feeling that grief is in the driver's seat can undermine this foundation.*

You have many helpers who are in spiritual form. When we are faced with a life crisis, it's as if angels and other spiritual beings gather at our door, waiting to be asked in. They are there to provide comfort, and hold the space for our soul's healing transformation. They await your request for assistance. Some people speak with angels, guides or other beings in spirit. Many have after-death communications with their loved ones through dreams, visions, auditory communication, "feeling their presence," and other ways. It is normal and healthy to talk with your loved ones in spirit form in whatever ways you are comfortable. They can be called upon when we need their support and reassurance. One of the more indirect ways that they help us is through books that we read. Have you had the experience of going into a library or bookstore, and you find just the right book, or perhaps it even almost jumps off the shelf into your hands? Or, a friend tells you about or loans you a book that speaks directly to your heart, just when you needed it. I don't believe this is coincidence. Your spiritual helpers will use whatever means they can to assist you and support your growth and development.

Years ago, two friends mentioned Johrei to me on two separate occasions. I barely noted this form of healing in my consciousness at

Reflection

Have you had the experience of going into a library or bookstore, and you find just the right book, or perhaps it even almost jumps off the shelf into your hands? Or, a friend tells you about or loans you a book that speaks directly to your heart, just when you needed it. I don't believe this is coincidence. Your spiritual helpers will use whatever means they can to assist you and support your growth and development.

those times. When the third friend brought it up, my ears perked up. I don't necessarily think it was because "the third time's the charm" but rather that I was "ready" to hear this information. I went to the Johrei Center and quickly realized it was a necessary part of my healing journey. Although it shared some similarities with other "energy" work such as Reiki or healing touch, I found this form resonated strongly with my whole being and helped me to connect deeply with my spiritual self. So be aware of the various ways your helpers may be speaking to you.

When we do take the time to try and communicate with them more directly, what often happens is that we do a lot of talking to spiritual beings, but then cut off any listening experience. We may believe that we won't be able to hear an answer anyway, so we pour out our hearts and leave it at that. For example, you might speak to your deceased husband and tell him your problem with your youngest child, and then you go off to feed the dog. If you can take a few extra minutes to sit quietly, sometimes an answer will come in the form of a thought, a metaphor or image, or an idea.

One of the places where I do my best receiving of information is in the bathtub! Water not only relaxes us, which can bring us to a more receptive state, but I believe there are properties of the water that assist this communication process. In her book *Water Dance,* (Paper Chase Press, New Orleans, 2000), Juliana Larson states, "And water can even induce altered states of consciousness, bringing us to a new and deeper understanding of who we are." (page 186).

Many of you are already connected to God through daily prayer and meditation. But in order to have a bridge to God, there has to be a two-way channel. Do the messages flow easily both ways? Whatever works for you—whether it is taking some deep breaths to help still your mind and not rush off to yet another task, or visualizing a stream of light from your heart to the spiritual being you are talking to—allow yourself to be open to "hearing" a response.

"The Voice of the Twilight" is a song about taking the time to *stop moving and doing,* and to *sit* in one place for a period of time and just *be.* When it is twilight, people and birds head home. One evening, as I sat on my back porch watching and listening, I was struck at how similar this part of the day was to meditation. With meditation or prayer, it is a time when we "go inside" in a different way, a time when we "return home." Each of us has probably had at

Reflection

When we do take the time to try and communicate with them more directly, what often happens is that we do a lot of talking to spiritual beings, but then cut off any listening experience. We may believe that we won't be able to hear an answer anyway, so we pour out our hearts and leave it at that. Instead, take some deep breaths to help still your mind and not rush off to yet another task, or visualize a stream of light from your heart to the spiritual being you are talking to—allow yourself to be open to "hearing" a response.

The Voice of the Twilight

As I sit, and watch sunset, and bid
    the day farewell,
Feel the gentle breeze cooling my
    skin, birds heading home.
Children, called in from their play,
    brush a kiss,
They bear the message of this wise
    old voice.

CHORUS:

It's the voice of the Twilight,
Calling us to go Inside, again.
Whispering to be Still, and Listen.

We are always looking for the
    answers from Without,
Searching for what we already
    know, just go Within.
All we must do is sit still, calm our
    thoughts, Hear Twilight's colors
    sing a gentle tune.

CHORUS

least one experience of feeling the stillness and exquisite beauty of twilight. And it is this feeling of peace and well-being that is ours also when we "go inside" our inner landscape. This song is a call to use this powerful and simple tool. It doesn't mean you must do hours of meditation each day. You can certainly do prolonged periods of meditation, but doing 5 minutes can build a connection too. The more consistently you build this bridge, the easier it is to become receptive. You can take a few deep breaths during a traffic jam and focus on your breath during those minutes that might otherwise be spent fuming or worrying. As you water your plants, keep your awareness on them and enjoy them rather than allowing your mind to distract you. You may call this "being in the moment." It *is* that too. Call it whatever you like, but take the time to *listen* as you do these things. Don't be surprised if you hear a message from your inner voice, or communications with your dog or cat. Maybe you will hear nothing other than your breath. That is good too. It gives you a break from the clutter of your day. Listen, and remember *who you are.*

Building a bridge to your higher self, that part of you strongly linked with God's Purpose, is strengthened by the same listening process. It is also encouraged when you take the risk to act on your intuition. We often hear the phrase, "listen to your inner voice." Or someone tells you to "trust your intuition or gut," or "follow your heart." How often do we do this? Some people paralyze themselves from any action, because they are afraid they are listening to their "ego," not their wise inner counsel. Others race from one thing to another because they think it is their inner voice sending them frantically in many directions. The key word in the instruction is "listen." *How can we hear anything, how can we be in touch with that higher part of our self unless we actually take the time to listen?*

I Park Myself on My Porch

What better place to engage in listening than your porch! Porches, or even a stoop, provide a place of resting from your activities and busy-ness. Choose a time when you don't have many family or work interruptions and sit, watch, listen and breathe. If you were to ask someone sitting quietly on their porch at dusk and watching the sky change colors and shapes what they are thinking about, many times it is "nothing." They are engaged in a form of meditation, a time of stillness, and quieting of the mind.

Most of us spend some time meditating, even though we don't call it that. We may sit at the kitchen table, sipping a cup of tea and watching the movements of a bird outside our window. Totally engrossed in this activity, we are unaware of anything else. Our thoughts have stopped their endless chatter, and the only activity in that realm is the thoughts or responses that are happening as we watch the bird.

So, yes, by all means, do pray and ask God and other beings for assistance with your grief, but also, take the time to listen. *To be quiet and still.*

AFFIRMATION 3: **Each day I build a bridge to my resources (God, spirit helpers, etc.) through prayer and meditation. I take time to be still and to listen.**

I Build a Bridge to My Human Helpers

Having a bridge to God, to your inner voice, and to other spiritual helpers is crucial, but not enough. You must allow other human beings to assist you during your grief journey. There are certainly days when we want to lock the door and not see another human being. That is normal and OK and we can ask other people to respect our need for this alone time.

One woman told me that after her son died, many concerned friends and family members were calling and dropping in. Although she appreciated their love and concern for her, she began to feel smothered and resentful. She took action and put a message on her answering machine on those days when she needed solitude. It said, "This is Mary. I am grateful for your call, and I need a couple of days to myself. Please don't call or come by right now. I am OK and will welcome your calls again soon."

Conversely, allowing yourself to go into seclusion and prolonged solitude is not a good idea. Each individual must decide what is the balance that feels right for her or him. However, *in general, you will benefit more from your healing process if you allow yourself to stay in contact with those who can listen to you when you need a compassionate ear, will hold you when you just need to cry, and will affirm for you that you are OK just as you are.* Support groups made up of people on similar healing journeys can boost your immune system, even as they assist you in repairing your wounded heart.

You will have people in your life who are not able to do these things for you, people who want to tell you how to live your life and how to manage your grief. They may want you to get busy and stay preoccupied so you won't have time to think about your losses and feel your feelings. Other people may be uncomfortable hearing about your pain or your thoughts. These people may have wonderful hearts and good intentions, but their effect may be more negative than positive at this time. It's OK to limit your time with them, or ask them to limit their advice and just listen. Know that at a later time, when you are feeling stronger and more whole, you can then choose to see them again.

A woman with breast cancer told me of her family's inability to let her have the time she needed to journey through the multitude of feelings that came with her diagnosis. They constantly told her to "Think positive, don't let it get you down, be grateful you're alive, stay strong, etc." It's not that these messages are terrible, but they didn't allow her the time she needed to get used to all the changes in her life. The timing was off. What she really wanted was their permission to feel bad for awhile until she was ready to move toward being more positive and active. Don't wait for anyone to tell you that you have a right to your feelings.

Meanwhile, while you are vulnerable and needing to use your energy wisely, build stronger bridges to the people who are making you feel that you are OK just as you are, that you don't have to "get over" your loss in any certain time frame, and people who are willing to walk some of this path with you. Even though you may recognize that these people are probably good for your health at this time, you may still be reluctant to spend much time with them. And that is OK, too. What *is* important is that you consciously make a stand with yourself that *you will not isolate*—that you will keep in contact with these life-affirming people, and that *you are willing to make the effort* to do so. Perhaps you will decide to make a time to see someone once a week, or you might ask another friend if they would be willing to go grocery shopping with you on a regular basis. Establish some agreed-upon times that you will interact with these people rather than leaving it to chance and desire. It takes much less effort to make a few set dates with these important people than it does to worry each week, "Oh, I should call Evelyn, but I don't want to bother her. Maybe she won't want to get together again this week. She's probably tired of my feelings and same-old stories." Evelyn will most likely be grateful that you want to include her in your healing, and the structure will assist her in feeling more useful too.

Pets are Powerful Resources and Healers

Do you have a pet? If you don't, seriously think about getting one, as they are some of the best healers on the planet. If you have a companion animal, you already know what a comfort they can be when you are feeling stressed, lonely or anxious. Many people believe their animals can understand a lot of what they say. I think mine also can read my mind much of the time. I believe they are special "angels" sent to assist humans to soften and to love each other and ourselves better. Talk to your animal friends about your feelings; share your positive and negative experiences with them. Ask for their help in becoming more peaceful and trusting of your process. Touch them with consciousness as you sit silently together. Give gratitude to them and to God for their presence in your life. *Think not only of building a stronger bridge to your pet, but know that they may also be a bridge, helping to strengthen your connection to God and other spiritual helpers.*

If you are grieving the loss of your pet, know that your connection with them can help you with this as well as other losses. Our society doesn't honor the deep love people have for their animal companions. As a grief counselor and presenter, I have found that many people tend to have the strongest feelings and reactions to my song about pet loss, "How Do I Say Goodbye," from my first book *The Joy of Grief.* I know their responses are a testimony to the strong bonds that form between humans and their animal companions.

Celebrate your connection to your present pets as well as those who have died. You know in your heart that they are important beings on the planet and contribute so much to your life. Don't let anyone shame you for your strong feelings for them. They are great gifts and wonderful teachers!

Nature is the #1 Healer

Nature is a resource that deserves a closer look. By nature, I am referring to the natural world—the earth, sky, wind, plants, animals

Reflection

I believe our animal companions are special "angels" sent to assist humans to soften and to love each other and ourselves better.

and minerals that make up our planet. A more conscious relationship with nature will increase your ability to have more joy. It will bring you to a more balanced position mentally, physically, emotionally and spiritually. Nature can be a bridge between you and God. ***Nature is a resource with the greatest potential to activate your self-healer.***

It is also one of the under-utilized healing tools at our fingertips. Just walking outside into your garden, or picking up a geranium pot and tending the flowers can be healing. Your *attitude* and *intention* can make the choice of nature as an avenue of healing more powerful. Being present and using affirmations to describe what you are doing can be very beneficial. For example, if you decide to "get some healing from Nature" and go outside with a stack of papers to grade, your awareness will be limited. Instead you can leave the papers for a later time and affirm, "I am making a choice for healing by taking time to nurture these plants and myself. I am grateful for the time I take out of my busy day to feed my soul!" *Be sure and take this extra step of affirming your choice for healing with your words as this presents an added layer to your healing.*

At one time it was considered very strange to talk to plants. Then research showed that plants that are talked to, sung to, or have classical music played grow better and healthier. I don't know if anyone has done the research on humans growing better and healthier *because* they talk to their plants, but I'm pretty sure it would support that idea. So whether you like to hug trees, read poetry to your rhododendrons, or serenade your stones (minerals, etc.), do so with love and intention.

You can thus **consciously** *choose to use time in nature to expedite your healing process. The only thing standing between you and an easier, more powerful healing is the way you prioritize your life.* If you live in a city, you will need to find more time to go outside the city to take a break from constant noise, pollution and stress, which are not conducive to healing. Even if you make time to be in your garden, you will need times to be away from the stressful influences of the city. Take a moment to remember the last time you went to the mountains, the desert, a secluded beach, or other place where you spent some peaceful and relaxing time. Can you remember the sweetness of sitting with *"bright yellow flower petals fresh with the dew"* or lowering yourself to the ground to smell the *"pine needles*

Nature's Gifts

Love opens me to Life today, Love
opens me to Life.
I feel an open-ness to grow, Love opens
me to Life.

Simple beauty gives my heart wings,
In each moment, my soul gently sings.

Bright yellow flower petals fresh with
the dew,
Pine needles scented in the sunlight's
warm glow,
Rainbows and sunsets, purple, gold, red
and blue,
Nature's gifts fill my heart to overflow.

scented in the sunlight's warm glow?" Does your body long for that place right now? Does your mind ache for the quiet and peace, away from telephones, televisions and other distractions? Does your heart sense the healing that awaits it in one of these places? Is your spirit already soaring towards that place in anticipation of the deep connections you can feel while there?

I can't imagine that you would say no to any of those questions. And yet, if you are like many people, you make time to have these experiences in nature rarely.

I know myself the benefits of nature's healing touch, yet I don't make this happen often enough. However, it's not helpful to introduce guilt into this equation. Why not make a deal with yourself to increase these times? Make it doable and easy at first. Perhaps you will promise yourself that on the 16th of this month, you will go to the mountains for the afternoon. But don't set yourself up for failure. You have to be willing to follow through with whatever commitment you have made. Maybe you aren't willing to leave the city yet. For you, maybe just saying "every Friday, I will walk the dog around the block" is what you are ready to do. After a couple of these sessions, your inner self is going to be so pleased that you took the time to nourish your whole being and that you followed through with your commitment. In turn, you will *want* to commune with nature more just because of the benefits you receive. Remember to give thanks to the earth, sky, air, water and whatever else you are appreciating. *The healing you are doing for yourself and the gratitude you express to nature can also contribute to healing the wounds of our planet.*

This relationship with nature can be one of the most wonderful gifts you can give yourself while you are grieving and, of course, even while you are not in grief. It can bring you more balance and joy than you could possibly imagine. You may want to take a journal with you to record your feelings and thoughts. Or you may simply want to enjoy the silence and the rest from "*doing*" and allow yourself the time to just "*be.*"

> AFFIRMATION 4: **I take time on a regular basis to go to nature and to enjoy what God has created. I am thankful for the times I do this and for the joy and peace it brings to my life.**

A Visual Tool: I Make a Resource Mandala

Making a list, a chart or a mandala of your inner and outer resources can provide a daily reminder of your commitment to live your journey in a more conscious way. Think of this as a representation of the ways you nurture your connection to your spirit, mind, body and heart. Some of my clients draw pictures or symbols alongside the words as a way to engage different parts of their brain in the process. A simple circle, divided pie-fashion, can serve to chart the numerous helpers you have on this journey. Don't forget to include the activities that bring you a sense of relaxation and well-being. Whether it is listening to music, reading inspirational literature, hiking, building birdhouses, quilting, eating chocolate or cleaning windows, make note of these nurturing activities. *Taking the time to make this chart is a strong message to your subconscious and to God that you have chosen to accept help and to stay connected with life.* Once again, make something that fits who you are, and post it where you will see it and enjoy it. If you are having a terrible day and can't

think straight, a chart in your drawer will not help to remind you of your "support team." It needs to be visible and prominent so that you will use it daily.

The example you see here was made by a woman who realized that her most precious resources were the ones she utilized the least: nature walks with her sweet animal companion, tending her flowers, spending time with friends, and silence and prayer during each day. Her mandala was in her favorite colors and she found that it served three purposes for her. Not only was it a reminder to take advantage of these areas of support, but also it uplifted her each time she saw it and it soon became a symbol of the ways she was nurturing herself. She began to feel better about herself and her ability to use her resources for healing.

Use conscious questioning as you make your mandala. "Who and what are my resources today?" Using these questions helps you to identify whether you are satisfied with the choices you are making and presents you with the option for change.

Step Three

I Surrender to, Trust and am Grateful for this Journey

Let's assume that you have agreed to take the first two stances. You have affirmed that you are willing to use this time of change and transition to re-create yourself and that you will build bridges daily to your resources. What's next?

Your third step is a combination of surrender, trust and gratitude. If you are like most people, when you are visited by a major challenge, you tense up and want to find a way to control what is happening to you. What I have seen in those most resilient with change is something different. There may be an initial "lock-up" reaction, yet the person follows this with awareness of the tension and a determination to relax the mind and body and enter willingly into their experience.

I Relax Into This Journey

This relaxation is a form of surrender. Let's look at my other definition of surrender. I remember watching cowboy movies as a child in the early 50's. The cavalry would raise the white flag of surrender as their battle with the enemy appeared hopeless. This is **not** the kind of surrender I am referring to. By surrender, I mean to "dive in" to your experience, to let go of the need to totally control every facet of your life, and to trust that you will learn and grow from it. To surrender is not about sticking one little toe in, and then the next, and so on. By diving in, you are showing God that you trust in the process, and that you have faith that you will not drown. And you won't, as long as you remember to continue to affirm and practice the first two stands. Just as with the stages of death and dying, you will go through these steps more than once. You must revisit them constantly in order to stay on track. But each time you practice them, you bring your process to a new level of healing.

"Diving in" requires being as present in each moment as you can be to the feelings and circumstances generated by the changes in your current life, rather than finding ways to escape them. It is about surrendering to this transformational process. For example, you may experience moments when you are flooded with difficult feelings. Allow them to course through you, rather than cutting them off, so they won't get stored in your body to come at you at a later time, or

Reflection

By surrender, I mean to "dive in" to your experience, to let go of the need to totally control every facet of your life, and to trust that you will learn and grow from it. To surrender is not about sticking one little toe in, and then the next, and so on. By diving in, you are showing God that you trust in the process, and that you have faith that you will not drown.

Reflection

If you don't surrender, you resist. To resist something is to fight it. It makes sense that if you are fighting something you are using energy that could be used more effectively for positive ends.

to cause some dis-ease. I refer here to something that takes away from a natural "ease" of living, that which introduces a block to wellness. Normally we shut down from experiencing our grief fully because we are scared. We don't trust that we can handle it. We have not surrendered to the process. To surrender is an act of faith and trust. It is not about giving up or an act of resignation. It is, on the contrary, an act of co-creation.

You can fully experience your grief and move through it with more ease by surrendering. If you don't surrender, you resist. To resist something is to fight it. *It makes sense that if you are fighting something you are using energy that could be used more effectively for positive ends.* Resistance to a natural process like grief creates more grief and dis-ease. Remember the saying, "What you resist, persists."

Try an experiment. The next time you have a wave of sadness come over you, quickly switch yourself into the surrender mode. Say a brief prayer for assistance from God, with your intention to accept the feeling and to allow it to move freely through you. Trust that you will be OK. Here is what has happened to people who have tried it: they had a different experience, one that felt more positive overall. Richard, a former client, was describing how he had rented a movie and was watching it at home when "The music in the background was so poignant and touched a nerve in me. I was picturing my son who was killed last year. I started to cry. I remembered what you said and took a deep breath and asked God to hold me while I cried. I told myself I was going to surrender to my feeling and that I would be OK. I cried hard for a couple of minutes and I didn't even stop the feelings by getting up to get a tissue. I felt the most wonderful warmth or peace as I finished. I really felt held by some unseen presence. Then I watched the rest of the movie and went on with my day feeling more relaxed." By surrendering to our feelings, we can remove some of the extra pain and grief that we cause ourselves.

Even when you have chosen to surrender to the process, there will be times when you make a choice to "shut down" your feelings, such as in a public place or in the workplace. Each situation is different and only you can make the right choice for you. Feeling and expressing intense emotions in the presence of others can cause discomfort and feelings of embarrassment. Treat yourself gently in this process of surrendering. Many of us have been "trained" to repress intense feelings so that fully surrendering is not a natural process. That's OK. Once again, stating your intention to yourself can assist you in opening yourself to greater expression.

A caution here. Surrendering to your feelings does not mean that you are letting the feeling "take over" or that you are willing to "become" or "be stuck in" the feeling. On the contrary, it is by accepting the feeling and feeling it fully that it can move through you rather than it taking residence in you or power from you.

If you are faced with a serious illness, to surrender does not mean that you must surrender to this illness. It is not a proclamation that you are giving yourself to the disease. It is rather a declaration that you accept that you have this illness as part of your life in this moment in time and that you are not resisting this fact or its lessons for you. By being more relaxed and open, you are better able to be open to guidance and treatment options that will work for you.

Fear No Longer Rules Me

Fear is one of those feelings that we do not like to experience and choose various ways to block and avoid it. The avoidance or denial of fear causes difficulties for many people. By allowing yourself to feel the fear and then to face it and take action, you take away its power. If you run from fear, it tends to set up housekeeping in your being. It becomes an unwelcome guest that becomes harder and harder to show to the door.

"What's Stopping You" is about acknowledging fear when it is present, feeling it move through you, and taking action with trust that you will survive. By feeling the fear and not allowing it to take over and paralyze you, you send a message to your whole self that you are capable, even when the going gets rough.

I Let Go of "Old Baggage"

The song "I Surrender" is about three life attitudes: *surrender, trust and gratitude* that can help you live your journey with less resistance, fear and pain and also to live your life's purpose. In my song, I speak about the process of letting go of "old baggage" such as beliefs, values and judgments that no longer serve your life. Surrender is a path of letting go, not just of control, but an inner-housekeeping that is often long overdue.

What's Stopping You?

What's stopping you from living your life
    more fully,
What's stopping you from opening to Love?
What holds you back from finishing what
    you started,
What makes you think that you're not enough?

Fears are feelings, they don't have to be
    your masters,
Look at them squarely, then even though
    you're scared,
You can do it, oh yes you can!

What's stopping you from taking those baby
    steps that,
Will lead you closer to your dream?
What keeps you from acknowledging who you
    are and,
That your Essence is much more than it seems?

Fears are feelings, they don't have to be
    your masters,
Look at them squarely, then even though
    you're scared,
You can do it, oh yes you can!

Fear can't rule me, I am strong,
With your Love, how can I go wrong?
I'll remember that it's ok,
To feel the fear,
And do it anyway.
To feel the fear,
And do it anyway.

Reflection

By allowing yourself to feel the fear and then to face it and take action, you take away its power. If you run from fear, it tends to set up housekeeping in your being. It becomes an unwelcome guest that becomes harder and harder to show to the door.

Surrender is an active state of awareness. In order to see what needs to be dropped, I must be conscious of what I believe and carry with me.

Do you like to keep the details of your life neatly ordered? You are not alone. The problem is that, when crisis hits us, an orderly life flies out the door. Because we have been in control of all these details for so long, it can be very hard to admit that we can't control them any longer. That's where trust comes in. If we surrender this control to God, and affirm that we trust that we will be guided through this unfamiliar territory, we have freed up an enormous amount of energy that was previously used to control our life experiences. Part of this trusting process is about listening for the guidance of the "still small voice" within, and then acting on it.

It is very freeing to not fight the energy of what is happening in each moment of our lives, but rather to work with it and trust that there is divine guidance at work. The gratitude expressed for what we **do** have and for what **is** working in our lives can bring balance to feelings of what **isn't** working. When you surrender and trust your healing process, you will find that some of the reclaimed energy naturally gravitates to feelings of gratitude. Not only are you grateful to not be in a worrying mode constantly, but also your vision has expanded—your glasses have changed so that you are able to see the gifts and daily miracles in your life. As you express your gratitude about what you have, you develop a deeper appreciation for life.

Oprah Winfrey's show has helped many to realize they have more choices available to them and that their spiritual self needs nurturing. She encouraged people to begin a "gratitude journal" that became a soul-saver for many. What a simple yet incredibly powerful act it is to say "thank you" or "I am grateful for…" This action helps to shift a habitual way of viewing one's world, which is often very negative and limited, to a practice of viewing one's world as rich, abundant, and full of things to be grateful for. Since many of us are already showing a negative balance in our worldview checkbooks, it does no harm to try and at least even things out. A practice such as a gratitude journal does even better. "I'm finding I feel more whole now…" is another benefit I refer to in my song. Not only does a gratitude practice help balance your life perspective, it also brings you closer to the desired wholeness of being. Thank you Oprah for affecting so many lives with your positive energy and ideas.

I Surrender

*I surrender, I let go and trust God's plan
    for me,
I am grateful, all my lessons are setting
    me free.*

*I'm tired of trying to manage, to control
    the things around me.
I'm letting go of old baggage that is
    binding and keeps me from feeling free.*

*I surrender, I surrender to God's
    loving hands,
I surrender, I surrender to God's
    loving hands,*

*I'd like to know all the answers, to see
    what the future will be,
I'm finding I feel much saner, when I'm
    trusting that inner voice totally.*

*I trust my life, I trust my life to God
    every day.
I trust my life, I trust my life to God
    every day.*

*It's easy to take for granted, all the gifts
    God's given to me.
I'm finding I feel more whole now, as I'm
    living each day much more gratefully.*

*I am grateful, I am grateful for my
    life today.
I am grateful, I am grateful for my
    life today!
I surrender to my life today!*

Reflection

When you surrender and trust your healing process, you will find that some of the reclaimed energy naturally gravitates to feelings of gratitude. Not only are you grateful to not be in a worrying mode constantly, but also your vision has expanded— your glasses have changed so that you are able to see the gifts and daily miracles in your life.

I Live My Life's Purpose

Lisa, the woman I mentioned earlier who made a conscious choice early in her grief journey to learn and grow from her experience, showed me another key to grieving with grace. Before her mother's illness and death, Lisa worked as an accountant for a small firm. She cut back on her hours in order to visit her mother more frequently in the nursing home. After her mother's death, Lisa continued to go to the nursing home to visit some of the residents. She told me that, although it was difficult to return to the nursing home after her mother's death, once she did, she felt an inner shift. "My heart began to open wider and wider to these elderly friends. I could understand my mother better and was able to forgive her for some past transgressions. Through these times at the home, I began to feel so much compassion for the elderly, for the person my mother was and for myself." Lisa had an intuitive flash one night before bed and was picturing herself working in the nursing home. She had some fearful moments but decided to trust her feelings and move forward. She quit her job, opened a small accounting practice from her home, and took a part-time position at the nursing home that had opened up a month after leaving her other job. "I feel like my mother's death and this grief journey are bringing me to my life's purpose. I have never felt more alive and my life more meaningful."

To "let go and let God" can bring you to your true self and your purpose. All human beings are "control freaks" to one degree or another. It's normal to want to steer our lives in the direction we think we should be going. In order to live our life's purpose, I believe we need to make room for God in the driver's seat. We may think we know where we're headed, but as is often the case, we are put on an entirely different road that leads us to more joy and satisfaction than the one we were on. A conscious question such as "In what areas of my life right now would I like to surrender more?" can help in this process. If you state to God that you are willing to live your life in a way that will be more fulfilling to you and those around you, you can then receive the guidance to do that.

Do you want to live your life's purpose? Do you even believe you have one? I think we have more than one. I believe that we all share one purpose: *to learn how to love each other and ourselves and live in peace and harmony on our planet.* That's a tall order, but one we

Reflection

All human beings are "control freaks" to one degree or another. It's normal to want to steer our lives in the direction we think we should be going. In order to live our life's purpose, I believe we need to make room for God in the driver's seat. We may think we know where we're headed, but as is often the case, we are put on an entirely different road that leads us to more joy and satisfaction than the one we were on.

can realize. Then, each of us has other life purposes, often more than one.

Don't worry if you don't know your life purpose. I am finding that a prayer is working for me, you know the one, "Lord, make me an instrument of peace…" I ask God to use me in whatever way will help me to fulfill my purpose, to guide me to take the steps that will bring me ever closer to being fully who God wants me to be. And then I let go, I breathe, and I surrender. I must be willing to go forward and act on the guidance I receive. I can't sit back and wait for someone else to do the work for me. It is a tricky balancing act to move forward with purpose and direction at the same time that you are constantly listening for those directions!

> AFFIRMATION 5: **I surrender to change and to my life as it is today. I trust that God is guiding me on this journey. I am grateful for each experience I have and for all the blessings in my life.**

I Can Have Gratitude for My Misfortunes

Many of you have already made a place in your heart for God and probably pray everyday. Often, these prayers are meant to ask for God's help and support for us and for the loved ones in our lives. There is nothing wrong with asking for help. It is far better than thinking we can "do it all alone."

However, the key to taking your life and your healing journey to a new level is remembering to work for *balance* in the things you do. So if you spend a certain amount of time asking God for help, it seems reasonable that you might also want to spend an equal amount of your time thanking God and giving back to God in service.

Can we have any gratitude for our challenges? When I was going through the incredible emotional pain of the aftermath of the attack, I was not thinking about thanking God for the "darkness" and for my grief. A wise woman, however, planted a seed with me that hinted at this possibility. Most people don't want to hear things like "Your grief will bring you great gifts eventually" or "There's a silver lining in every cloud" while they are in great pain. Timing is crucial, and hearing these statements from others is not always helpful.

Reflection

Gratitude is like soothing balm to your soul. It gives the message to your inner healer that you are willing to focus part of your day on the positive aspects of your life, and not give in to just negative thoughts or painful feelings.

However, when *it's your own life and your own loss, you can be in charge of planting these seeds.*

Experiment with creating some balance for yourself in the way you view your pain and loss. Try talking to God about it, about how you would like to trust that this change in your life has a purpose and that you are grateful to God for leading you towards peace, compassion and understanding. Try thanking God for all your life experiences, as painful as some of them may be. Pay attention to how you feel each time you try saying these things to yourself. Also, remember that during this time of your loss, you may have conflicted feelings. You may want to shout, "No! I'm not grateful at all that you took away my husband! As a matter of fact, I'm so angry at you God that I could scream!" Don't tell yourself that you are a bad person to have that thought. It's OK to get mad at God. Can you imagine anyone else being able to handle your anger better than God? The worst thing you can do at this point is to put yourself down. Say what you need to say, either out loud, or write it down, letter-style. Or perhaps you have anger surfacing at someone else. It's all OK. They are only feelings. Let them out and they will then pass. They won't be able to be tucked away in some corner of your mind until you get to the bursting point.

Even though it's more difficult to have a "gratitude practice" while you are in the midst of pain, *remember that gratitude is one of the most powerful transforming agents that we have at our disposal every day.* Most of us use this life enhancement to some degree, but there is so much more to it than we know! So, as you encounter new losses, remember that there is a plan for you and your life and that you are right where you are supposed to be. Allow the possibility of saying "thank you" for your particular trials, and trust that each step you take brings you to a deeper healing.

Gratitude is like soothing balm to your soul. It gives the message to your inner healer that you are willing to focus part of your day on the positive aspects of your life, and not give in to just negative thoughts or painful feelings. But gratitude is not just about saying thank you to God or other helpers not in human form. It is about connecting to yourself and to others in a more life-affirming and expansive way.

There are many ways to make gratitude an everyday occurrence in your life. As mentioned before, there is the "gratitude journal" in which you write several things each day you are grateful for. Others like to sing songs of praise to God during the day. Someone else may write special notes of thanks and appreciation to friends, family or colleagues. Don't forget the power of the spoken word! Remember how you feel when you receive heartfelt thanks for something you have done? We want the process of gratitude to become habitual, but *the actual expression requires thoughtfulness, heart and clear intention.*

I Create a Better Balance of Positive and Negative Self-Talk

Being grateful to God and others is not enough, however. You may thank everyone around you for being wonderful and helpful but never say a word of kindness to yourself. *This is a step that you cannot afford to skip or take lightly.* **You must show gratitude to yourself in order to grow and find balance.** You will not learn to love yourself and others fully until you begin to acknowledge yourself for all that you do. It's not enough for others to say their thanks to you. You have to tell yourself how wonderful you are!

How often do we do this? We may pat ourselves on the back occasionally and give a high five to someone when we've just done something we're proud of. Is this enough? No! While the gestures such as patting your shoulder as a symbol of "good job" are helpful, they don't go far enough in transforming your inner landscape. You must voice to yourself what you are grateful for. Let me give you some examples.

Most of us pass up thousands of opportunities to tell ourselves positive things about what we do, say or think. But we find a myriad of occasions to give ourselves a hard time for not being perfect or for messing up. "I can't believe I forgot to mention those statistics during my presentation. What was I thinking?" No mention is made to oneself that everything else about the presentation was great and enthusiastically received by the attendees. Do we tell ourselves anything for having done a good job, even if it is a routine one? Not usually. When you are taking time for yourself, such as a warm bath, tell yourself, "I am taking time alone to heal. I have given myself the gift of this precious bath. Good for me!" Or as you sit at a traffic light having just completed a breathing exercise, finish it by telling yourself that you have just made a choice for healing by using that time to do breath work. You've just put the kids to bed and are washing

Reflection

Being grateful to God and others is not enough, however. You may thank everyone around you for being wonderful and helpful but never say a word of kindness to yourself. This is a step that you cannot afford to skip or take lightly. **You must show gratitude to yourself in order to grow and find balance.**

the dishes. You think about what you *should* have said to your boss that day, or what you *should* have done when you were feeling confused about a decision you made. Balance these thoughts with what you did right. "I am proud of myself because I had the courage to speak up to my boss and alert him to the problem. Tomorrow's another day and I can follow up this conversation."

The point is, we don't create a balance in our minds between the negative and the positive. Tell yourself that you are going to give yourself as many, if not more, positive as negative messages.

Sometimes we are not aware of our negative self-feedback. One trick to increase your awareness is to keep a "basket of positive messages" and a "basket of negative messages" for a few days. Take buttons or small stones and put them in a bowl in front of the baskets. When you catch yourself thinking positive thoughts about yourself or your life, put a stone or button in the positive basket. "I'm going to try that new activity even though I'm a bit anxious." "I did a nice job with my hair today." "I was able to fix that leak myself!" Likewise, when you become aware of a negative or draining thought, place one in the negative basket. "I can't do this." "I'm too dense to get that." "I can't believe I said such a stupid thing." At the end of each day, take a look to see how many are in each. Do they balance each other? As you do this exercise more and more, you will become more aware of this balance and be able to automatically correct it in the moment.

Giving yourself more positive feedback may feel awkward at first, but that's only because it's new. Try saying some of your praise aloud to yourself. Look in a mirror and give a smile with it. OK, that may not be your cup of tea. But, at least give it a try. The important thing is that you begin to love yourself the way God loves you. God notices all the wonderful things you do. As you begin to praise yourself, it will become easier to notice and to praise others. You will be creating a more balanced praise system. It's not enough to praise God each day and to thank others for their contributions. And it's not enough to remember to give yourself appreciation. You must do all three.

AFFIRMATION 6: **I am grateful to God, to myself and to others for my life, for my experiences and my growth. I take time each day to praise God, myself and other people.**

Reflection

In fact, this process of uncovering ourselves is a real treasure hunt. If we can remind ourselves that it is a process rather than the product or goal, and that we don't have to be perfect in our self-education, then maybe we stand a chance of being happy and joyful along the way.

Reflection

A wise teacher once said, "You don't have to be a master musician (or a master anything) to share your gifts with the world. Each one of us, warts and all, has talents, qualities or abilities that will assist the healing of self and the world."

Step Four

I Learn to Accept and Love All Parts of Myself

Giving oneself appreciation can feel strange and unnatural. We are usually born with what it takes to have a positive self-image but it needs to be nurtured by those around us. Yet by the time we are adults (for some, sadly, it happens while they are still quite young), many of us are afraid of admitting just how unworthy we feel inside.

The fourth stance to make on this journey is one of self-love and acceptance. Do you ever get tired of hearing that you have to learn to love yourself before you can truly love others? Are there times when you don't have a clue as to what that phrase means or how to go about making this elusive thing called self-love happen? You're not alone.

I remember having a revelation at a workshop I attended where this concept was brought forward. I felt panicky inside and thought "Oh my, she says that we shouldn't be in relationship with others until we learn to love ourselves. Now, not only should I not be in relationship until I clear up all my issues from the past, which in itself is at least another 30-year process, but I also have to undertake another process that sounds pretty foreign to me. Well, Marcia, you might as well write a farewell letter to family and friends, book a passage to a remote island and spend the rest of your life in seclusion, old girl, because all that work will take more days than you could possibly have in this lifetime." I felt pretty glum about the whole love business for a while. However, my longing to be in a relationship turned down the volume of these "experts" and I continued my usual "trial by fire" method of "learning to love." What I didn't understand was that I was not living in a black and white world and that there was *room for loving while learning to love.*

I think that we often lose sight of the fact that it took each of us years to layer ourselves with our insecurities, our dysfunctional behaviors, and limiting thoughts and beliefs. Yet we expect to dump them all in one fell swoop, or even two or three. In fact, this process of uncovering ourselves is a real treasure hunt. If we can remind ourselves that it is a process rather than the product or goal, and that we don't have to be perfect in our self-education, then maybe we stand a chance of being happy and joyful along the way. Allow that during some moments in your days you may be judgmental, out of

Learning to Love Myself

Gazing deep inside myself, and accepting all I see,
It is the lesson of learning to love myself, and be
*   the best I can be.*

CHORUS:
Learning to love myself, just the way I am today.
It's a lesson of letting go, and it's called The Heart's Way.
Learning to love myself, just the way I am today.
It's a lesson of gratitude, and it's called The Heart's Way.

Every human soul I meet, is a mirror for learning,
Whatever shadow I see in another person, is a
*   reflection of me.*

CHORUS

Finding balance in my Life, means accepting all of me,
When I let go of perfection and be more present,
I feel whole and set free.

CHORUS

balance, afraid, or stifling your feelings…you get the picture. If we allow ourselves the room to be human as we strive towards being more fully loving and compassionate, then we enjoy this unfolding of the true self so much more.

Learning to love yourself is a lifelong lesson. As you feel yourself letting go of ways of perceiving and acting in life that no longer serve you, give yourself gifts to celebrate your progress. On those days when your "dark side" makes an appearance, offer this part of you love and compassion. The "dark side" or "shadow" refers to those parts of yourself that you hide as well as you can because you feel they are unacceptable. For example, these aspects could be your anger, fear or other "negative" qualities. The shadow can also contain parts of you that are dimensions of yourself that you hide

---

To Be Gentle With Myself

To be gentle with myself, is my prayer, is my prayer,
To be gentle with myself, is my prayer.
For when I am kind to me, I can be more kind to you,
To be gentle with myself, is my prayer.

To be grateful for my Life, is my prayer, is my prayer,
To be grateful for my Life, is my prayer.
For when I am thankful for, all the lessons that I live,
I am honoring my Life, as a prayer.

---

because you don't feel worthy. For example, if someone told you earlier in your life that you had a terrible voice and shouldn't sing, you would probably refrain from singing in the company of others. Or perhaps you admire the courage of others to take risks, but feel you are not as capable as them. You hide your courage in your shadow self and project it onto others. Each part of you contains hidden gifts and is assisting you in becoming all that you can be.

My Shadow or Dark Side isn't So Dark After All

Accepting your shadow or dark side is another one of those statements we hear all the time. It is an important step to loving oneself that can be easily overlooked. Here's a great tool to assist you with accepting and integrating your shadow side. I call it the "magic mirror."

Whenever I come across someone I meet or know who annoys me or makes me uncomfortable, I ask my "magic mirror" for more information. This mirror is simply my *willingness* to see how this person is reflecting some quality of mine that would like to be acknowledged. My belief is that these people are great gifts and teachers for me on this journey of self-acceptance. Whatever you are judging in the other person is usually a quality in yourself that hasn't been accepted and integrated. It is calling for your attention.

For example, I get irritated by people who are judgmental of others or myself. When viewed in my magic mirror, I see that I really

Reflection

Whenever I come across someone I meet or know who annoys me or makes me uncomfortable, I ask my "magic mirror" for more information. This mirror is simply my willingness to see how this person is reflecting some quality of mine that would like to be acknowledged. My belief is that these people are great gifts and teachers for me on this journey of self-acceptance. Whatever you are judging in the other person is usually a quality in yourself that hasn't been accepted and integrated. It is calling for your attention.

don't like that critical part of my own personality. When I hear someone criticizing another or telling me what I did "wrong," I now look for the gift in this interaction. I need to ask myself, "Where in my own life am I being overly-critical or judgmental?" Many times, these negative qualities in others and ourselves are just strengths gone amuck. The part of me that is critical of myself or someone else can also be seen as my powers of discernment, which are often accurate about people and situations. If I let this gift get out of hand—by using it with the wrong intention, little to no awareness, or with bad timing—it becomes harmful. If I can love and accept this part of myself that has the strengths of honesty, integrity and the desire to be helpful, I can more easily reel it in with awareness. This process also assists me in being more compassionate towards those who are being critical in my presence. *The shadows or dark aspects of ourselves, when mirrored in love and compassion, are really not scary or awful at all. They are gifts that only need acknowledgment, acceptance, and conscious choice to use them with love instead of fear.*

You'll know you are making progress in this area when some of the buttons that used to get pushed have become neutral. You no longer need to draw to you the people who will mirror your "unacceptable qualities."

AFFIRMATION 7: **As I learn to love myself, I see that I am a wonderful work-in-progress. I can love all aspects of myself, including those shadows, which are gifts in disguise.**

Step Five
I Make Life-Affirming Choices Daily
Which Create More Balance

I Reduce Guilt in My Life

The path of self-healing may seem impossible when you are feeling that your fears and shadows may overtake you and drown you. To surrender to your grief and to your feelings doesn't mean you have to give yourself and your identity over to your feelings. There is a difference between allowing yourself to *feel* deep pain and despair and allowing yourself to *become* despair. The same thing goes for guilt. Everyone has regrets after a loss and some guilt about what they could have done differently. Whether it's a job you have lost, your health, a loved one, or a part of your identity, everyone thinks about the *"if onlys"* and the *"should haves."* "If only I had listened to my doctor back then, I wouldn't have cancer now." "I should have kept him home instead of letting him go out with his friends." "If only I had spent more time with him, he'd be alive now." After my assault, I was plagued with "if onlys." "If only I hadn't been hiking alone." "I should have taken a different trail." "If only I had gone straight to work." But all this self-talk did was dig my hole deeper and make the recovery longer. It's not that we won't have these feelings and guilt-ridden thoughts. **But we *can* choose to do less of it!** The way to transform this guilt is to do so consciously. You can reduce excessive guilt by re-framing it. For example, rather than beat myself up by saying, "If only I hadn't taken that hike," I could choose to say something like: "I made a healthy choice to take a hike on that beautiful day. I used the information available to me and made the best possible choice I could. While on that hike, a terrible and traumatic thing happened to me. I allow myself to grow and become a better, more loving person as a result of that event. I am choosing to use any remaining guilt energy for my higher purpose, not as a drain on my energy." Take the stand, "I let go," ask for God's help, and make the choice to use your guilt energy constructively: to re-construct your life with more purpose and joy.

This next song, "Should'ng on Myself," takes a light look at the guilt process we have been talking about. When we overdo the "shoulds" in our self-criticism, we are dumping on ourselves, littering our inner landscape with emotional doo-doo. We can instead allow ourselves to be human and thus imperfect.

The fifth step of the Heart's Way process is to make conscious CHOICES of how you use your energy in your thoughts, words and actions so as to create more balance. Balance is a state of equilibrium, where there is neither too much nor too little. You hear people talking about balance all the time: "I'm having a hard time balancing my checkbook." "I can't seem to balance my home life with my work life." "I'm going to balance my yin and yang."

Of course we all want balance in our lives, especially when the rug has been pulled out from under our feet. And, when the things that

Should'ng on Myself

Well I get up everyday and I try to do my best,
Make the choices that are healthy, eat good foods and
    lots of rest,
Yet I can't begin to tell you what a struggle this can be,
Discipline takes a vacation and my judgment gets whacky.

Well I shoulda gone to workout so my muscles don't
    go slack,
And I shoulda chosen carrots, not those corn chips for
    my snack,
And I shoulda sat in lotus 'stead of talking to my friends,
But I get so doggone weary, always trying to make
    amends.

CHORUS:
I'm a should'ng on myself way too much, don't you think?
With all this should'ng everywhere I must be raising quite
    a stink.
Well I'd better clean my act up, 'fore the shouldas hit
    the fan,
Take a breath and just relax girl, You're doing the best
    you can.

Well, I shoulda drank 8 glasses of pure water yesterday,
But it's really way too boring and who's counting anyway?
Yes, I shoulda ordered tofu, but it's pizza I did take,
And I shoulda gone to church, 'stead of baking chocolate
    cake.

Well I think it's pretty obvious that the lesson of this song
Is that should'ng's not too healthy, makes your life a bit
    less long,
The solution to this problem is to constipate your guilt,
Take out oughta, shoulda, have to, live from joy and
    be fulfilled.

you counted on before to bring you balance are no longer there, how in the world do you create equilibrium where there seems to be a constant earthquake occurring?

Through practicing awareness of your choices, you can search for and find balance. A word of caution, however, is in order. Not everyone has the same balancing point. Just as each healing journey is different, each person must find the ways in which to balance his or her thoughts, words and actions and life. Also balance is not static. Like life, it is ever changing. What may be a point of balance for you today may need to be adjusted tomorrow. Flexibility and balance are partners.

What happens when we are grieving and not thinking about balance? We are then at the mercy of the process. We are sitting around waiting for each wave and then mopping up the mess afterwards. *But if we proactively tell ourselves that we are going to try to do a check and balance of our daily experiences, then we send a message of power, not of victimization, to our mind, body, heart and spirit.*

We can make choices that are *life-giving* rather *than life-depleting* and defeating. **The four kinds of choices we will look at are: choosing love over fear; choosing light and lightness or humor over "sweating the small stuff"; choosing kindness over meanness; and choosing to expand rather than contract.**

I Choose Love More than Fear

I am not suggesting that we won't make fear-based choices ever again. Of course we will. What we can do, though, *is to create a different balance in our choices.* We can decide to make *more* choices that are based on love, acceptance and connection, and thus *less* choices that separate us from ourselves and others.

The thoughts that you think, whether they are the "if onlys" and other guilt-related thoughts, have a profound effect on what kind of life you live. Many of us have been waiting for our lives to get better. We wait for our luck to change. This is similar to the hope that many people share that life will be paradise after they've died and left this mess called "Life on Earth." They are living out their lives, almost in a fog, holding onto the promise of a better life in "heaven." But let's imagine for a moment, a different scenario. Let's try on a new pair of glasses.

What if heaven is right here, right now, and we just don't see it?

Reflection

Each and every thought you think has energy. It travels through the atmosphere, similar to sound and light waves, and has an effect on yourself, those around you, and those far away.

What if we could have Paradise on Earth, and not put any worry into what comes later. Maybe if we make heaven on earth while we're still in human form, our Paradise on the Other Side will be even that much more heavenly! *Because we have changed our inner landscape.*

Is this possible? Absolutely! What do people say about heaven, the ones who've had the near-death experiences? They say it's beautiful, clean, clear, with brilliant colors, incredible light and filled with absolute peace.

So how do we do this on Earth? Of course it's good to focus on cleaning up our environment and trying to undo the damage we have done to our Mother Earth. This is a necessary aspect of creating paradise. However, *the real clean up begins inside.* We have to clean our inner landscape daily with awareness. As you clean, which means paying attention to your thoughts, words and actions and discarding those that are fear-based and no longer serve you, you will feel not only brighter, cleaner and more beautiful inside, but you will attract to you situations and people with similar brighter energy.

Each and every thought you think has energy. It travels through the atmosphere, similar to sound and light waves, and has an effect on yourself, those around you, and those far away. Think about a time you were in the presence of someone who was angry with you but wasn't saying a word. Their energy was palpable and you probably felt like moving farther away from them.

Most of us aren't even aware of how often our thoughts are fear-based and negative. There is often an internal monologue that is often engaged in criticizing oneself and others, sometimes in very subtle ways. Try the following experiment. Those who have done so have said it was an eye-opener to a process that was usually habitual and invisible. They found that simple awareness became the key to their transformation.

Follow your thoughts and words for a few days. Use a notebook and divide a page into 3 columns: *Love, Fear* and *Neutral* (neutral is a questionable possibility, as love and fear cover most situations; however, if you are unsure, use neutral for those you cannot identify). For each thought that you think to yourself or verbalize, make a check under the appropriate column. For example: (1) You are rubbing your temples and wishing your headache would go away; this goes under *fear*, as you are fearful it might stay; (2) You say hello to a colleague and compliment them on a report they did; this goes under *love* if you are truly appreciative of their work, or under *fear* if you are merely saying it to earn points with them; (3) Your daughter asks you for help with her homework; you do it grudgingly but inwardly you are wishing you were working on your own things. Which column? *Fear.*

It is normal as you undergo major change to have what we term "negative" thoughts. There are many unknowns in the weeks and months ahead that bring fear and doubt to the surface. As you are faced with intense feelings of sadness, guilt, anger or despair, you will have times when you are thinking critical thoughts about yourself or others. It is important that you are gentle with yourself and not "beat up on yourself" for having them. The key to not becoming victim to these thoughts is to *acknowledge* them, *commit to your intention to be in the moment,* and *choose love over fear.* If I allow myself to constantly return to the "should haves," I am choosing to remain stuck in the past. If I am worrying constantly about what is going to happen in the future, (such as "How will I ever do what I need to do?"), I am choosing fear rather than trusting that I am safe and that I have help with my life journey. I have not surrendered. After you have reviewed your intention, you can balance any critical thought you just had with a positive one, about yourself or the other person. For example, let's return to the two sisters on their unique grief journeys after their mother died. Sarah operated almost exclusively on a fear level. When she had thoughts or feelings about her mother's death she would squelch them with "I can't go there. It will kill me. I have to put that behind me." When she did seek some help about a year after the death, she was constantly going over and over what she could have done differently to prevent the death. "If only I had watched her more carefully. I would have picked up that she wasn't feeling well and gotten her to the doctor sooner. I should have been more forceful about her taking better care of herself..." Although these thoughts can be normal grief responses, they became a problem for Sarah as they continued too long and began to interfere with her present life. She was unable to put into perspective all the good things she had done for her mother as well as being unable to accept her mother's death. On the other hand, Lisa responded differently. Although she too had some initial guilt and "if onlys" to work through, they were more easily released as she was balancing her life with positive thoughts as well. She was able to say, "I wish it could have happened differently, but Momma had a hard illness and it's been hard for me. There are things I could have done that may have been better for her and for me, yet overall, I am proud of all I did for her. I gave a lot of my time to be with her during her illness and I helped her to have what she needed as she was dying. I really did the best I could at the time. I have learned from watching her that there are things I can do to take better care of myself. I'm proud of myself for taking small steps to keep my mind and body healthy. I'm certainly doing a better job of that than before her illness." Lisa continued to observe how she was changing and growing from her grief journey. Sarah, in contrast, resisted change and tended to dwell on negative thoughts. I have found that positive thoughts have a cumulative effect, as do the negative ones. Why not try to shift the energy in a more love-filled direction?

> AFFIRMATION 8: I create Paradise on Earth today with the thoughts I think. I choose to be more aware of my thoughts and to choose with love more than fear.

I Support the Lightness in My Being

"Light in My Soul" is about choosing to open our hearts so that the light (*LOVE*) in our soul can shine and grow. The more you sing this song to yourself, the more you will feel your heart softening and opening. *Through repetition, these songs, just as the affirmations, have the power to assist you to build habitual ways of thinking and being which support a unified and healthy spirit, mind, body and heart.*

To choose lightness is also the choice for a different perspective on minor life challenges. Having a crisis or major challenge in one's life affords us the opportunity to put things in perspective. Will your life really fall apart if you don't do the dishes tonight instead of playing a game with your children? When another driver cuts in front of your vehicle, you can choose to wave them on with good humor because you've made a conscious choice to not *"sweat the small stuff."* On second thought, don't wave at all to them as this can be misinterpreted too easily. A nod and a smile will do. An incredible internal shift takes place as you begin to automatically weigh the importance of various events and activities. It becomes more auto-

---

Light in My Soul

There is light in my soul, in my soul.
And the key to this light is my Love.
For when I open my heart,
The love can flow in, the love can flow out.
It's a choice that I make for the Light, for the Light.
It's a choice that I make for the Light.

There is light in your soul, in your soul.
And the key to this light, is Your Love.
For when you open your heart,
The love can flow in, the love can flow out.
It's a choice that you make for the Light, for the Light.
It's a choice that you make for the Light.'

---

matic at some point to pick the things that nurture the highest expression of yourself and to discard those that would not serve your growth.

To me this song is also about the choice for humor. Humor that is neither mean nor about separation, but rather for joining, is one of the powerful assistants in your healing journey. Celebrate this part of yourself and nourish it with play. If you don't have any young children in your life right now, choose ways to be around some. Join with them in silly games and thoughts. Rent the movies that take you to a place of lightness. And as you laugh, affirm to yourself that you enjoy laughing and that it helps you to heal.

Practice laughing. Do you know people who have some of the heartiest and fully expressed laughs on the planet? If you are not already one of these people, imitate them when no one is looking. Practice really can help. Listen to the "Laughing Exercise" and join us as we play with different forms of laughing. When you begin trying on different ways of laughing and giggling, even though you may begin by pretending to laugh, you will almost always end up with genuine laughter and smiles. Think of it as a practice, just as meditation or breathing techniques become disciplined practices and part of your lifestyle.

AFFIRMATION 9: **I am lightening up. I choose more and more not to "sweat the small stuff." I choose ways to exercise my laugh muscles as a tool for self-healing.**

So, lighten up my friends. Laugh at and with yourself as you climb your mountains and slide down some valleys, and know that in doing so you are sending a wonderful message to those around you. You are being a mirror of a Divine Human Being!

I Can be Kind or Mean

It is sometimes easier to see the effects of our words rather than our thoughts. When I was growing up a popular chant on the school-yard was *"Sticks and stones may break my bones, but words will never hurt me."* You probably recognize that too. This was a magical phrase that was supposed to help us deal with hurtful things other kids might say to us. Although our physical bodies weren't invincible, our emotional bodies were supposed to be. But, when you're a kid, you don't have the same "mythical" powers as adults. I found that the words often hurt much more than the physical pain and lasted a whole lot longer! As a young child, I not only didn't understand this saying, but I made a serious misinterpretation one day. I thought it meant that if someone *did* hurt you with their words, then you were justified in using either sticks or stones on them. A little boy named Ron got a stone in the middle of his back after yelling something mean at me!

Many of the people I have worked with over the years talk about how words spoken to them decades ago still can float up to the surface of their consciousness and wound them all over again. They can feel the hurt, not just emotionally or mentally, but also on a physical level. One woman told me how her first husband used to belittle her, telling her she was worthless, incompetent and unlovable. As she spoke these words 20 years later, she clutched at her chest and spoke softly, finding very little breath to support her speech. Those words had wounded her, not just emotionally, but physically. We all know the connection that exists between the body, mind, heart and spirit. It should be no surprise that the words that we say to others affect them on more than one level.

"Sticks and Stones" encourages us to be more conscious of the words we speak. "My words can heal and my words can wound...I always have a choice." As we create our new self, this is one step we can take to become more the angels on earth that we were meant to be. This step is not about getting down on ourselves for saying something we regret later, or feeling we have failed if we don't always say positive things to everyone. When you are in turmoil yourself, you will have times when you feel that everything you say is the wrong thing. You may hear yourself being negative and critical. Your awareness is the first step to making some changes. It's OK to occasionally slip and say the wrong thing. It doesn't mean you are a bad person or that you will never feel or act differently. You are in the process of awakening. This step in our awakening is about *choice.* It's about paying more attention.

Not only do we need to pay attention to *what* we say, but to *how* we say it. My daughter calls me on this one from time to time. She will say, "It's not *what* you said Mom, it's the *way* you said it." Usually if we say something that has an edge to it, or use a tone of voice that alters the way the person hears our words, it is because we aren't telling the truth. Our words don't match with the intention. If our intention is to be kind, the words will ring loud and clear. If we want to wound someone, that will come across also, even if the words by themselves are neutral or positive. Sarcasm is a perfect example of this type of wounding.

If our intention is to heal our hearts (and by extension, Mother Earth's heart, and the heart of the Universe), then it pays to be kinder to each other. If is helpful to take a moment to breathe before we say something unkind. Ask yourself the question, "In this situation, how can I say what I need to say, in a way that comes from love, not fear?" This requires daily practice. With time, you can do this less self-consciously, and more habitually. Even when we have very difficult feedback to give to someone with whom we are having problems, it can be done in a respectful way.

Be kind to yourself above all! If you slip and say something to a friend or loved one that *is* hurtful, by all means apologize, and then move on. If you use that slip-up as an excuse to beat up on yourself ("You idiot, there you go again, you're supposed to be forming your words from love not fear, you'll never get it, you're too dense," etc., etc.), then you may need to take more breaths not only before you speak out loud but to yourself!

Sticks and Stones

CHORUS:

*Sticks and stones may break my
    bones,
But words can never hurt me.
That's what my mother said to me,
But my heart did not agree, oh no,
My tender heart could not agree.*

*My words can heal and my words
    can wound,
As I use my voice,
Well I can build you up, or I can,
    tear you down,
I always have a choice,
Oh yes, I always have a choice.*

*Sometimes we'll slip and we'll say
    some things,
That hurt the ones that we love,
But there are four good words for
    us to remember,
I'm sorry and I forgive,
Oh yes, I'm sorry and I forgive.*

AFFIRMATION 10: **I pay attention to the words I say because my words are powerful. I use my words to heal, not wound, myself and others.**

I Can Expand or Contract

One of the greatest gifts that you can receive from your healing journey is an awakening. This is merely an expansion of limited vision and of your spirit. You will awaken to who you were meant to be on this earth. I know that if you are reading this, you have already awakened to a degree. After each major loss that you experience, you have the chance to awaken a little bit more, or a lot more, depending on your willingness to embrace the process. You can become aware of the treasures within you that have been waiting to shine forth. Take advantage of this opportunity to discover your Divine Essence.

To choose expansion over contraction is a willingness to explore your boundaries and beliefs about life, this world, and worlds beyond the one you can see in front of you. How do you do that? First I can tell you how not to bring an expanded awareness into your life. Surround yourself with negative people, sit in a messy, dirty room with dark colors around you, hardly ever go outside in the fresh air, don't listen to any music, and certainly don't dance or do any movement other than what is necessary. Those are just some of the ways to ensure a joyless, limited existence.

Now, let's see about the other avenue, about developing a more expansive and joyful life. We've already covered the idea about thinking more positive thoughts and having more positive people around you. What's wrong with a messy, dirty room with dark colors? People who live in messy, dirty, cluttered spaces usually mirror this internally. Chaos inside will breed chaos on the outside and vice versa. Think about a time when you cleaned up a particularly messy area in your house. You sorted out some things, threw away what was unnecessary to keep, scrubbed some 5-year old dirt away here and there, and created a tidy, sparkling area. Do you remember what it felt like to be in that spot, as opposed to the pre-cleaning feeling? Make no mistake here about the type of cleaning I am referring to. Those who are "compulsive cleaners" and can't stand to have a spot of dirt or a hair out of place are not "expansive cleaning." They are

Reflection

After each major loss that you experience, you have the chance to awaken a little bit more, or a lot more, depending on your willingness to embrace the process. You can become aware of the treasures within you that have been waiting to shine forth. Take advantage of this opportunity to discover your Divine Essence.

cleaning out of a need to control their inner chaos and do not usually do the inner housekeeping that is necessary to a healthy and balanced lifestyle.

When we clean up our environment on the outside, such as in our house or our yard, there is usually a corresponding emotional and mental clean-up happening. As we sort through and discard the material belongings that no longer serve us, we become aware of things in our inner and outer life that no longer serve our highest good and can be let go. It is as if the space and order you have created around you have also done the same thing for you on the inside. And, when you create order and space in your inner landscape, you *make room for more joy and more positive feelings to come in.* There is no room for you to have more joy in your life if you have filled it with mostly negative clutter.

I Choose Color as a Healing Tool

Next, let's briefly discuss color. Color is one of those things that we take for granted. Look around you at home. What colors have you used to decorate your house? What color clothes do you wear? What colors make you feel really good?

While attending a non-traditional university, a section of one of my courses was devoted to our emotional response to color. Part of our coursework was to sit or lie in various small meditation rooms, each a different color, and observe our responses, whether they be physical, mental, emotional or spiritual. Many people in my class had similar thoughts, feelings and memories evoked by certain colors. You could use the power of this exercise in your mind. Relax yourself as you do before a visualization and then see yourself in a red room. Allow yourself to just "be" in this image for a period of time. After noting your responses, either on paper or into a tape recorder, then picture yourself in an orange room, and so on. What have you learned about yourself and color from this exercise?

Numerous studies have been done on the effects of color on our moods and our health. There are many books available at your library or at the bookstores. I suggest you go look at a couple of them and begin to pay closer attention to this helpful health activator. I'm not talking about the books that deal mostly with "your colors," or the colors that suit your skin and hair color. While there are helpful principles in those books as well, I am referring to the books that deal with the effects of certain colors on your body, mind, heart and spirit. Included in theses are books that take a look at the colors associated with the energy centers, or chakras, in our bodies. So, experiment with wearing different colors, and notice what the colors in nature do for you. Then, when you see you are attracted to certain colors, take time to sit with them, look at them and absorb them into your very being. Don't forget to say thank you to the Creator for this wonderful aid for balance. Be sure to tell yourself something like, "I am becoming more aware of and using color and beauty for my healing."

I Use Music, TV, Food, Sound, Breath and Movement Consciously for my Healing Journey

We can also choose expansion utilizing the power of music for healing. Perhaps you have found that when you are grieving, a certain song can touch you so quickly and so deeply, that you begin to cry no matter where you are. This can be very disconcerting when it happens, but it is normal. Music is more than a cathartic catalyst. Music can help you to clean your inner landscape, connect with joyful feelings and be a bridge to your inner self, God and your spiritual nature.

Music is made of vibrations, actual waves of energy, which move through your body, mind, heart, and spirit and have an effect on each part. Music can help to activate your immune system response, be as powerful a mind-clearer as meditation, and help your heart and feelings to soar. It can also have the opposite effects and bring chaos and dis-ease to your being. So, it's important to choose music that makes you feel good. That's pretty simple. If you notice during the day that the radio is playing something that grates on your nerves, turn it off. Don't allow it to play, even if the volume is turned down. It will have a negative effect on you, even at low volume.

The same thing goes for TV. Notice how you feel when you are watching various programs. Does the program make you feel good? Do you feel more agitated or tense as a result of watching it? Some people keep the TV on in the background as a simple form of company. This is not always a good idea because you are being affected by the music, the other sounds, and the content of "lower-vibrational" commercials, news and programs, whether you are actively watching it or not. I worked briefly with a family whose young children were having severe behavioral problems. When I came for a home visit, not only was the TV on in the living room, but in the bedrooms as well. The mother informed me that she kept the TV on in the kids' room 24 hours a day "to soothe them." Imagine the amount of stimulation, not to mention inappropriate programs that were influencing these children's bodies, minds, hearts and spirits.

I'm not saying that you need to turn off your TV forever (although it's tempting sometimes, isn't it?). Remember, we are talking about balance. Why not be more pro-active in creating a healthy, peaceful atmosphere in your living space? Have the TV on only when you want to watch certain programs that you enjoy. Watch less of the news programs, as they are usually very unbalanced in presenting positive and negative stories (which produce more tension and less well-being in you). Taking these simple steps can produce immediate and profound change in your sense of peace and balance.

I need to mention the vibrational aspect of food. It is well known that if we choose to eat food that is rich in nutrition and low in additives or pesticides that we will be healthier and feel better. Many people are still eating a diet that is rich in junk and poor in nutrition despite this knowledge. Once again, I'm talking about balance. Being a purist in your food selection may work for you, but if it doesn't, that's OK too. Choose to eat healthily most of the time. Lower vibrational foods cannot give you what you need to be fully alive, vibrant and fulfilling your potential. Occasional choices of these foods when you have committed to eating well the majority of the time can be part of a balanced lifestyle.

Let's get back to the effects of music and sound. You may already be familiar with the therapeutic effects of music, but did you know that sound is a healer too? From the simplest yawns and groans to a more complex chant, sounds from your own vocal chords are bridges to health and wholeness. When you sing along with your favorite tunes, you are increasing the breath (oxygen) available to your body and you are promoting health in your spirit. Your being is in an expansion mode. Unfortunately, many people say they can't sing and rarely do it, even privately. They have been told by someone along their life path "to be quiet," "you can't carry a tune," and then they begin to believe this lie. Their throats and spirits contract as a result. If you are able to make a sound, you can sing. It is healing to do so.

Reflection

From the simplest yawns and groans to a more complex chant, sounds from your own vocal chords are bridges to health and wholeness.

You can increase your joy just by taking deep breaths each day and letting them out with a big sigh, Ahhhhhh! That's simple enough, isn't it? But you can go to various levels with this: learn about toning, take a vocal workshop, or simply experiment with your voice in your morning shower. Don't worry about making pretty noises; just make any kind of noise and sound. Feel the vibrations in your body as you do this. Notice how your ability to breathe more deeply is increased. You will probably notice emotional and spiritual benefits as well. And this healing tool is available to you at any moment during your day.

Using the breath consciously is an amazing expansion tool. This could be doing a simple breath exercise before prayer or meditation. Or give yourself the "gift of breath awareness" while sitting at a traffic light. Breathe in for 4 counts, hold your breath for 2, and then exhale in 6 counts. This is only one of many ways to activate this powerful healing tool. Regular breath exercise practice can expand your connection to God, to those "mysteries of life," and to feeling healthier in all parts of your being.

When was the last time you danced with joy? With abandon? Have you ever allowed your body to move to music just the way it wants to while no one is watching? Having studied dance/movement therapy for a number of years, I found that initially, my body would only move in the ways that were expected of it—from years of conditioning and watching other people move their bodies. But as I stripped away those layers of conditioning, I found that my body has an unlimited repertoire of movement. Try a simple experiment. Put on one of your favorite musical pieces, sit in a chair and shut your eyes. Just move your hands in response to the music. Let them do anything they want. You can open your eyes at some point and watch them if you'd like. You could even imagine that they are dancing partners and see what they would do separately and together. The point is, your whole body can do what your hands just did. They can create movement and energy with very little equipment— just a little music and privacy. Maybe you feel you can't move or dance because you have limited physical capacities. Perhaps you are confined to a wheelchair. Even if all you can do is blink your eyes because the rest of you is paralyzed, your eyes, and your inner landscape can dance. I've worked with people of varying abilities, and **everyone** can dance. *If you choose to do so.* Whether you just tap your toes to a tune, or you get up and really "cut the "rug," go ahead and let your body have its way and you will find that you are more wide awake!

> AFFIRMATION 11: **I choose to expand my experience of life. I surround myself with wonderful colors, music and experiences that give me pleasure. I allow myself to move my body, whether it is through dance, exercise or deep breathing. All these increase my ability to have more joy and balance.**

I Contemplate the Mysteries of Life

What is one of the greatest mysteries of life? I think it is the question of where we come from before we are born and where we go after we leave our human body behind at death. Why is this such a mystery? Because most of us haven't developed the ability to "walk between the worlds"—in other words, to visit the spirit realm at will. And many of us don't believe the accounts of the ones who have or who speak to spirits and gain information that way. For many people, if you can't see it or touch it, it isn't real.

It's just another frontier, and many people are opening their minds and hearts to all kinds of possibilities. At one time, people didn't believe that the world was round, that there were people living on the other side of the earth that looked and talked differently from them, or that there were microscopic creatures living on their own skin. They didn't believe in anything they couldn't see for themselves. However, the times, they are-a-changing. Who knows how many things exist that we still don't see!

At this point in history, we're in the midst of a spiritual revolution. And this spiritual revolution is actually moving closer *to* rather than further *away* from the scientific and technological revolution that has enveloped us this past century. Physicists are speaking about other "dimensions" and opening themselves to acknowledging that there is more to life than we have traditionally viewed. More and more people are reporting experiences that can't be scientifically proven. Just about everyone has their own story about something miraculous that happened to them or one of their family members, where there was some unseen helper during a crisis situation. Stories about angels have become best sellers because people have an inner recognition of their truth and power.

Are there angels and spirit guides assisting humanity to remember who they are? I believe so with all my being, and for me, it has taken years of growing and reading and experiencing synchronicities and "miracles" daily in order for me to know this. It is a question each person will answer for her or himself. But, if you're still sitting on the fence, all you have to do is say a prayer and ask for help to find your answer. Then, be aware of all the "coincidences" that you begin to notice, and allow yourself to be open to new ideas. I don't believe in coincidences and have heard that word defined as "A God-guided event in which God prefers to remain anonymous."

Part of the following song has to do with nature and the mysteries that are within all the amazing creations on our planet and beyond. It is truly mind-boggling to contemplate the intelligence that creates everything from an intricate flower to the Aurora Borealis. This song is a call to us all to celebrate these mysteries. And though I refer to life after death in the song, I intend for us to contemplate other mysteries as well. Some of these are synchronistic events in our lives, the birth of a child, the accounts of peoples' past lives, the great variety and beauty in Mother Nature, and the most amazing mystery of all: the power of love.

To expand is to adopt new perspectives and to see as "gifts in your life" those events you may have previously viewed as annoyances, inconveniences, or even tragedies. As you grow, you begin to feel more gratitude and celebration for what you have at this moment in time. Your whole self begins to trust more that each lesson that comes to you is assisting you in becoming happier and more alive. You have less of a tendency to forget that you were created with a spark of divine wonder and magnificence.

As already discussed, nature can enrich your healing journey. Give yourself the gift of putting on many different pairs of glasses every day. Part of choosing expansion rather than contraction is the willingness to "try on" someone else's perspective. When you hear someone telling a story that seems too fantastical to you, take a breath, and then tell yourself, "wait, there could be something to this. I'm going to pretend for a minute that this is totally true. And I am going to see how I feel about that possibility."

My husband recently visited Iceland. While there, he took a special tour that visited the places where the "hidden people" live.

The Mystery of Life

Do you believe that you die,
When you take your last breath?
Is that the end, is there no more,
No life beyond, what you have known
    on Earth?

Too many people have died,
Without looking beyond,
What they could see, in front of them,
They needed proof, that there was
    something more.

CHORUS:

Take time every day, to explore the
    mystery of Life,
Be sure to look beyond, what you
    have known,
What you can see and hear.

Don't be surprised if you find,
Many things magical,
Will come to you, as you expand,
Your mind and heart, there'll be no
    turning back.

Look for the gifts in your Life,
Celebrate what you have,
And take each lesson, as it comes,
And don't forget, your Essence
    is Divine.

According to the people he spoke to there, about 70% of the population believe in the hidden people. The mayor of the town of Hafnarfjorour writes the following on a map given to those on the tour, "In Hafnarfjorour, we have known for a long time of another society coexistent with our human one, a community concealed from most people with its dwellings in many parts of the town and the lava and cliffs that surround it. We are convinced that the elves, hidden people and other beings living there are favorably disposed towards us and as fond of our town as we are." How do you feel about this possibility? I don't know about you, but I am putting Iceland on my list of places to visit.

It is only fear that makes us turn away from something that is not part of our everyday belief system. However, human beings are finally realizing that we limit ourselves to knowing our world by just using the usual five senses. There is so much more to life than we know. We can develop other ways of perceiving our world.

What kinds of angelic or paranormal experiences have you had? Most people report having had some sort of "strange" happening. For some it was a "feeling that a spirit was there." Or "I shouldn't be standing here talking to you right now because I was almost killed that night. I still don't know how that car missed me!" Or, "I felt the most wonderful warm feeling come over me." Or "I had the weirdest feeling that something had happened to my son, and then I got the call from the sheriff's department." Working in the bereavement field, I have had client after client relate their experiences of having some form of after-death communication with loved ones. What a wondrous mystery!

We have many helpers in the spirit realm. The more we acknowledge this and thank God for these "angels," the more we can increase their healing potential in our lives. If you are feeling the loss of a loved one, you have probably already had thoughts about whether this person is now alive in spirit form. Do you ever talk to this person? If you do, you are normal as the countless others doing the same thing. Many of you probably have felt that your loved one may have been helping you from the "Other Side." They probably are. Take the time to add them to your prayers. I believe those in spirit form can benefit from our prayers for their continued joy, peace and growth, just as much as we benefit from their ministrations for us.

AFFIRMATION 12: **I celebrate the mysteries of life. I open my spirit, mind, body and heart to connect more deeply with these mysteries.**

Step Six
I Tend My Soul's Garden Daily

One of the sweet mysteries of life is the ability of humans to begin each day as if it were "the beginning of the rest of your life." Of my clients who seemed to have the least stressful healing journeys after major losses, this attitude was a common denominator. Each of them was able and willing to move beyond perceived difficulties from the day before and make a commitment to be open to new solutions and fresh perceptions. This attitude also assisted them in being pro-active about their well being in their everyday life. They were able to create more balance in their lifestyle with awareness of their choices and maintained healthier bodies, minds, hearts and spirits as a result.

The sixth step in this transformational journey is to make a commitment each day to tend your soul's garden. "Each day of life is a precious gift" begins the last song in this book. Even when we are faced with life-shattering challenges, this gift needs our attention and gratitude. Each day is a new day and brings the opportunity to begin with a fresh slate. It is very important to see each day as a fresh start, a new beginning. By making this thought more conscious on a daily basis, you make a pathway to enable the fifth step of choices to settle in and have a container for working.

A *"fresh start"* implies that you will be *doing* something and you will be taking *action* to nurture your growth and transformation. This step is your willingness to be a leader rather than a follower. You are the master gardener for your growth (well, co-master gardener along with God) and will be making daily choices about the things that will feed your whole being's evolvement. You will be faced with many decisions about what people, activities, books, treatments and information to invite into your life and healing journey. Every good gardener knows that part of the process is experimentation and that many factors contribute to a successful garden.

A successful gardener also knows that the daylight and nighttime are both important to the growth of plants. Such is the case also with

Beautiful

Each day of life is a precious gift, on this journey
   to be whole,
May you tend your garden so carefully, that
   houses your sweet soul.
Life is beautiful, plant seeds of hope and love,
Life is beautiful, sing compassion like the dove,
Let go of the past, live this year like it's your last,
For life is beautiful, to me.

The winds of change and the challenges can
   bring us to our knees,
Practice gentleness, patience with your growth,
It's one of love's great keys.

You are beautiful, there's light within your soul,
You are beautiful, even broken you are whole,
You deserve the best, to be loved with respect,
For you are beautiful, to me.

You're an angel, there's so much you can give,
You're an angel, Now is the time to live,
Kindness is a choice, use your life, your gifts,
   your voice,
For you're an angel, to me.
Life is Beautiful, to me.

your soul's garden. We need both the darker times and lighter, more joyous times to bring the seeds for new life and growth to birth and eventually to flower. The cycles and seasons of nature are great teachers in this gardening of the soul. Sometimes the gestation period is longer than we would like. Know that if you have planted the seeds and are nurturing them, they will grow.

I Listen for Inner Guidance

Part of your gardening job is to remind yourself to listen to your inner guidance. For some this inner knowing comes through a body sensation that they've come to recognize as their "gut reaction." Others become acquainted with a "little voice" that says "yes, I think that's it" when presented with an option. I was in the garden shop one day asking how to discourage bugs from eating and destroying our grapevine. I was given many options and felt kind of dizzy from all the information being presented. Faced with so many choices on how to proceed, you must remember to take time to breathe, ask for guidance and listen. So, after the clerk/gardener had regaled me with his incredible knowledge and expertise, I replied with a dazzling response, "Do you have a restroom I could use?" I took time in that "rest room" to take a rest from the information, to breathe and to ask my higher self which option was the best for the garden, the grapevine, the insects, my family, and the earth. As soon as I asked myself the question—after the breath and intention preparation—the answer was there. The more you trust that "still, small voice," the easier the process becomes.

I Mend My Fences

You've heard the expression "mend your fences." Your soul's garden needs fences that are sturdy and in good repair. When we have harsh words with someone, there are times when we don't come back later to say we're sorry or work things out. Sometimes days, weeks, months, and even years go by before we take care of these hurt feelings. They will stay inside our bodies until we make the choice to do something. If it is not feasible or in your best interests to make amends with the person involved, you can do so in your mind. You can picture them and yourself meeting and make up the conversation of healing. Especially be sure to forgive yourself in this conversation for any harm it has caused you. Be aware of your intention and use this imagery or conversation to connect rather than to blame and separate. Remember the "magic mirror" and be conscious of the shadow aspects involved in some relationship problems. In this way, you "sing compassion like a dove," as I phrase it in my song, "Beautiful."

"You deserve the best, to be loved with respect," pertains to receiving respect from others, and also from yourself. As you learn to love yourself, you will find that you draw to you people who are more respectful and loving towards you. Even while mending fences, you are aware of setting boundaries that encourage healthier relationships. You no longer allow yourself or others to deplete you.

I Make Choices for Growth

The concept of choice is key to being a successful rider of the waves of change. Even if you think you did a lousy job with the choices you made yesterday, today is a new day and a new beginning. Each day we make the best choices we can with the tools and information we have. Yes, by all means learn from these choices and then let them go. Make a conscious effort each day to be grateful for the opportunity to begin anew, to select the options that will further your soul's growth.

It is hard to know what decision to make at times. I have certainly left some "weeds" in my life's garden for far too long. I have also planted new seeds that never seemed to grow, whether they were ideas, friendships, or new activities. You will never be totally certain about all of your choices. What you do is make the space and time to listen for your inner voice's guidance, make the best pick you can with the information you have available, and then do it! *If you are still having trouble with your decisions, sing this song over and over.* Your angels will surely connect with your intention more strongly!

I Cultivate Compassion and Patience for my Growth

After I finished this manuscript, I allowed it to sit in the computer for a year while I let this material play more fully in my life. I began to work on the songs in the recording studio. I also consciously chose to practice the steps outlined in this book. What I discovered was that forging new habits is not easy for me. I found myself certainly doing all the things I know to be supportive of my spirit, mind, body and heart—but I also saw myself doing them less

Reflection

You've heard the expression "mend your fences." Your soul's garden needs fences that are sturdy and in good repair. When we have harsh words with some-one, there are times when we don't come back later to say we're sorry or work things out. Sometimes days, weeks, months, and even years go by before we take care of these hurt feelings. They will stay inside our bodies until we make the choice to do something.

Reflection

You will never be totally certain about all of your choices. What you do is make the space and time to listen for your inner voice's guidance, make the best pick you can with the information you have available, and then do it!

Reflection

We are all works-in-progress, and as long as we are taking steps to become more of our potential, we are moving forward. As always, whenever you are making changes in your life, one of the best things you can do for yourself is to be patient with your progress. Be kind to yourself, accept your weaknesses and know that each step, however small, is leading to more wholeness, to a more beautiful garden.

often than I would have liked. In other words, I wasn't disciplined in my approach and would do a little bit of this and a little bit of that. I was not following the approach consistently day to day.

But I also began to notice some changes in myself, positive ones. My awareness of my choices was growing. I *was* taking more time to breathe and to pray. There was growth in all areas even though I wasn't doing everything perfectly by the book. I was making progress. That's the point isn't it? We are all works-in-progress, and as long as we are taking steps to become more of our potential, we are moving forward. As always, whenever you are making changes in your life, one of the best things you can do for yourself is to be patient with your progress. Be kind to yourself, accept your weaknesses and know that each step, however small, is leading to more wholeness, to a more beautiful garden.

Know that in your core, you contain divine love and that you are watched by a loving band of spiritual cheerleaders who support you when your steps falter and applaud you when you leap and take flight. Fly with me my friends, and set your soul free!

AFFIRMATION #13: **I take time to tend my soul's garden on a daily basis through the choices I make for growth and life. I see each day as a clean slate with infinite possibilities. I am patient with my soul's progress.**

A Review

We have just traveled through six steps, that, when acknowledged and practiced with intention, will empower you to meet any change in your life with more confidence and trust. I invite you to embrace these steps on your healing journey. What you have to gain is more connection with your spirit, mind, body and heart. These six aspects do not define your self-healing journey, but rather allow you to move back and forth between them with flexibility and skill. You will see that they are practical guides for daily living as well, and with practice can become habitual. As you face incredible changes and challenges in your life, you can meet them with faith and trust that you will survive them and *be transformed in positive ways by their energy* (step 1). As you strengthen your *bridges to your resources* (step 2), you will feel more power and energy available to you to be a co-creator of your life with God. You can *trust* this journey of transformation and *surrender to* the process, to your feelings and to your inner guidance. You cultivate an attitude of *gratitude* that strengthens your ability to *"dive in."* (step 3). Your self-confidence and relationships will improve as you learn to *love yourself* better (step 4). Being more *conscious* of your daily *choices* will bring more harmony, balance and less stress into your inner and outer lives (step 5). By making a commitment to being a *gardener of your soul* daily (step 6), you send a message of hope, faith and trust to your higher self, to God, and to the world around you. You are signaling to your whole being that you expect a harvest, and that your gardening efforts will pay off.

I Become an Angel on Earth

This brings me to the last thought for this book. Angels are not just "in heaven." We are born with the potential to be warm, compassionate and loving human beings. To bring more balance into your life, you have to be *giving out at least as much as you are receiving.* Every day we receive love from the universe through the beauty of our plants and flowers, from friends and family who take the time to stay connected with us, from the kindness of complete strangers, and good thoughts and prayers from others that we never even know about. You must take the time each day to *give back in kind.* Sending prayers and kind thoughts for others is a place to start. Even when you are grieving, you can do little things for others. I know there are days when you have nothing in you to give to other people, when you don't even want to see anyone's face. It's OK to have those kinds of days. You can still be giving on those days with your thoughts and prayers. Of course, you must be sure to include positive thoughts and prayers for yourself and about yourself. On a day when you have a little bit more energy, write a nice card to someone you haven't seen in a long time. Maybe this person did you a nice favor, or maybe they didn't. It doesn't matter. Just practice some random acts of kindness and your ability to receive love is going to grow. **You will find that through these acts of service, you will begin to have days when you are feeling more energy and more connection to life!**

Most of all, give thanks to God that you are alive and that you appreciate all that you have in your life. If you stay focused too long on what is lacking in your life and all the difficulties you have day to

---

Reflection

By making a commitment to being a gardener of your soul daily, you send a message of hope, faith and trust to your higher self, to God, and to the world around you. You are signaling to your whole being that you expect a harvest, and that your gardening efforts will pay off.

---

day, you will create even more difficulties and more loss. If you make it a habit to increase your praise for what is going *right* in your life, for the gifts you receive daily, then you will find these things increasing. It really works! As my song says, "Use your life, your gifts, your voice, you're an angel to me." I do believe that each of us is an angel on earth with so much to give. Each of us has gifts to develop and each voice has important contributions to share.

My song also challenges us to "live this year like it's your last." This is such a freeing concept and one I hope you can embrace. If you clearly state to yourself, "I am going to live this present year as if it is my last year on earth," you will be choosing a path of great love and awareness of the gift of life. An aid to this journey would be Stephen Levine's book, *A Year to Live: How to Live This Year as if it were Your Last*. Taking time to journal your thoughts and feelings as you travel through your "last year" will add to the power of this growth.

It is up to you to choose how you respond to change and what kind of healing journeys you are going to have. You are co-creating it every moment of every day. Why not choose a path that brings you to more joy, more purpose and more of your divine self? Why not take a good look at your life as you have lived it up until now and see whether you could improve upon it? What is stopping you from becoming exactly who you were meant to be? Absolutely nothing. Certainly not change and grief. Gather the energy from these times of challenge, work *with* the wind, and utilize it to grow in ways you never thought were possible.

Let the window of your heart and your mind open as you read my words, and the words in other books that are most certainly going to come your way. Be prepared for a *Transformation.* It will take time, as all transformations do, but it *is* happening at this very moment. Take the time to listen to the yearning of your soul to be whole. Listen to the music that goes with this book to support the new pathways you are making in your brain and your life! I wish you each a blessed journey to your true self.

Reflection

If you clearly state to yourself, "I am going to live this present year as if it is my last year on earth," you will be choosing a path of great love and awareness of the gift of life.

Reflection

Know that in your core, you contain divine love and that you are watched by a loving band of spiritual cheerleaders who support you when your steps falter and applaud you when you leap and take flight. Fly with me my friends, let the winds of change lift your wings, and set your soul free!

The Winds of Change

CD CREDITS

1. The Winds of Change
Bunny Kirby – *lead vocals and guitar*
Marcia Breitenbach – *background vocals*
Johanna Volkert-Nelson – *cello*
Mike Kuhn – *flute*
Michael Fan – *violin*

2. We Are All Rainbows
Marcia Breitenbach – *lead vocals and piano*
CHILDREN'S CHOIR: Stefanie Frost, Alice Glasser, Alexis Higbee,
   Ariana Nicolini
Jess Hawk Oakenstar – *spoken introduction*
Lisa Otey – *synthesizer*

3. The Voice of the Twilight
Bunny Kirby – *lead vocals*
Marcia Breitenbach – *piano*

4. Nature's Gifts
Bunny Kirby – *lead vocals and guitar*
Marcia Breitenbach – *piano*
Johanna Volkert-Nelson – *cello*

5. What's Stopping You?
Bunny Kirby – *lead vocals and guitar*
Marcia Breitenbach – *background vocals and piano*

6. I Surrender
Bunny Kirby – *lead and background vocals*
Marcia Breitenbach – *keyboard*

7. Learning to Love Myself
Marcia Breitenbach – *lead vocals and piano*
Bunny Kirby – *background vocals and guitar*
Gillian DeLear – *drums*

The Winds of Change

CD CREDITS

8. **To Be Gentle With Myself**
   Marcia Breitenbach – *lead and background vocals*
   Bunny Kirby – *background vocals and guitar*

9. **Should'ng on Myself**
   Marcia Breitenbach – *lead vocals and piano*
   Bonnie Miller – *background vocals*

10. **Light in My Soul**
    Bunny Kirby – *lead vocals, guitar*
    Marcia Breitenbach – *background vocals*
    Gillian DeLear – *percussion*

11. **Laughing Exercise**
    Marcia Breitenbach, Marcey DiCaro, Alice Glasser, Bonnie Miller
    and Jess Hawk Oakenstar – *laughing fools*

12. **Sticks and Stones**
    Marcia Breitenbach – *lead and background vocals and piano*
    Damaris Drewry – *background vocals*
    Gillian DeLear – *percussion*

13. **The Mystery of Life**
    Bunny Kirby – *lead and background vocals, keyboard and guitar*

14. **Beautiful**
    Marcia Breitenbach – *lead vocals, piano and synthesizer*
    Bonnie Miller – *background vocals*

All lyrics and music written by Marcia Breitenbach

Music engineered, mixed and mastered by Gillian DeLear
at Southwest Sound, Tucson, Arizona

For more information about

Marcia Breitenbach's books, CD's and workshops,

WRITE TO:

Bridges to Self-Healing
4165 W. Ironwood Hill Dr.
Tucson, AZ 85745

SEND A FAX TO:

(520) 743-8502

E-MAIL:

marciab@theriver.com

To order a "My Angels" t-shirt,
call (505) 471-4100.

Notes

Notes